POVERTY, INEQU
AND SOCIAL W(

The impact of neoliberalism
and austerity politics on
welfare provision

Ian Cummins

apa Reference
Intext : (Comming, 2018)

Cummins, I. (2018). Poverty, inequality
and social work: the impact of
neoliberalis and austerity politics on
welfare provision. Bristol, United
Kingdom: Policy press.

P

First published in Great Britain in 2018 by

Policy Press
University of Bristol
1-9 Old Park Hill
Bristol
BS2 8BB
UK
t: +44 (0)117 954 5940
pp-info@bristol.ac.uk
www.policypress.co.uk

North America office:
Policy Press
c/o The University of Chicago Press
1427 East 60th Street
Chicago, IL 60637, USA
t: +1 773 702 7700
f: +1 773-702-9756
sales@press.uchicago.edu
www.press.uchicago.edu

© Policy Press 2018

British Library Cataloguing in Publication Data
A catalogue record for this book is available from the British Library

Library of Congress Cataloging-in-Publication Data
A catalog record for this book has been requested

ISBN 978-1-4473-3482-8 paperback
ISBN 978-1-4473-3480-4 hardcover
ISBN 978-1-4473-3483-5 ePub
ISBN 978-1-4473-3484-2 Mobi
ISBN 978-1-4473-3481-1 ePdf

Cover design by Qube
Front cover image: Shutterstock
Printed and bound in Great Britain by CMP, Poole
Policy Press uses environmentally responsible print partners

Acknowledgements

Isobel Bainton, Helen Davis, Shannon Kneis, Ruth Wallace and all the staff at Policy Press have been unfailingly supportive of the project. Thank you.

This work is based on my social work practice, teaching and academic research. I would like to thank my social work students who have listened to and helped shape my ideas. I am very grateful to the anonymous reviewers of the original proposal and a draft of the work. Their contribution has been invaluable in shaping the final version. I was honoured that Dr Emily Keddell and Dr Jo Warner – two social work academics I hold in the highest regard – took the time to read a draft of the book. I, of course, take full responsibility for the final version. Thank you.

My pals on Twitter (some of whom are real people) – @asifamhp, @SchrebersSister, @Hannah_Bows, @bonklesoul, @AcademicDiary, @BenHCarrington, @DrImogenTyler, @Stephen_A_Webb – you have helped in shaping my ideas in a number of areas that are explored in this work. Thank you.

The work of Paul Michael Garrett has been a key influence on my approach to these issues – if only he could be encouraged to write more.

I am particularly grateful for the support and encouragement of my friends Janet Chapman, Emilio Jose Gomez Ciriano, David Edmondson, Akwugo Emejulu, Marian Foley, Jameel Hadi, Stephen Jones, Gavin Kendall, Martin King, Jadigwa Leigh, Jane Lucas, Bernard Melling, Bryn Morris, Lisa Morriss, Emma Palmer, Kate Parkinson, Donna Peach, Dave Platten, Nick, Platten, Sarah Pollock, Barry Schilling and Jonathan Simon.

I would like to thank my sisters, brother and late mother for the support they have given me. My mother loved books, and I hope that she would have enjoyed this one.

This work is dedicated to my wife, Marilyn,
and to my sons, Nelson and Elliot.

If we had a keen vision of all that is ordinary in human life, it would be like hearing the grass grow or the squirrel's heart beat, and we should die of that roar which is the other side of silence. (George Eliot, *Middlemarch*, 1863)

Contents

List of tables and figures

Tables

Figures

Foreword

As Simon Fuller wrote in his introduction to *The Poetry of Protest* in 1991: 'In some situations the art of writing is itself a protest'. In the situation we find ourselves now, in which inequality has risen inexorably after decades of neoliberalism and years of austerity, we need to protest through all the means we can muster.

In April 2017, a group of social workers protested against the politically-driven austerity measures of the last two Governments, and the social and human devastation they are leaving in their wake, by walking 100 miles from the head office of the British Association of Social Workers (BASW) in Birmingham to the venue of its 2017 conference in Liverpool. The idea for this walk emerged from reading other pages that first documented and then inspired protest, namely an article by Psychologists Against Austerity published late in 2016 by the *Critical and Radical Social Work* journal. The social actions described in this article included 'Walk The Talk', in which a group of psychologists walked from the offices of the British Psychological Society in Leicester to offices in London to raise awareness of social policies that were leading to psychological distress.

Almost as soon as I had finished reading this article and put the journal to one side, I checked my 2017 calendar and the distance from Birmingham to Liverpool. I shared the beginnings of my idea with BASW colleagues and their positive responses led to the birth of Boot Out Austerity. We would walk an average of 15 miles a day for seven days, holding rallies and meetings each morning and evening, and visit social care organisations affected by austerity along the route.

We gathered at the yet-to-be-opened new BASW head office on Waterloo Street in Birmingham on Wednesday 19th April 2017, the day after Theresa May had called a snap General Election. She said she wanted a mandate to take into the soon-to-begin Brexit negotiations, whereas the Boot Out Austerity walkers were not alone in believing the key electoral battles would be fought on the fields of austerity, poverty and inequality.

One of the most egregious effects of austerity has been the huge increase in rough sleeping, with a quadrupling of the number of rough sleepers in Birmingham over a six year period, and some had been bedding down for the night outside the empty building BASW was to move into. We had chosen a theme for each day of the walk, a particular field affected by austerity, and on that first day we focused on housing and homelessness. The opening rally included speakers from the Axe

The Housing Act Campaign and Birmingham Christmas Shelter, who laid bare the impact of the reduction of available social housing, welfare reform and benefit cuts on meeting this most fundamental need for many of our fellow citizens.

We heard from other speakers too, including from the International Federation of Social Workers, the local BASW branch and the Social Workers Union. And there was music, political songs from the Banner Theatre and a piece composed especially for us by a student from the Birmingham Conservatoire, A Blast for Boot Out Austerity! The morning rallies on the other days were all in a similar vein, with poetry added in to the mix, one of the walkers reading out the daily poem written by our resident Poet Austeriate about the previous day's theme and happenings.

Having held our rally we would set off together, a core group of eight who walked the whole way, joined by varying numbers of others each day, from a small handful between Wolverhampton to Stafford, to the more than fifty who marched together through the streets of Liverpool towards the Pier Head on the final afternoon. Of the many crucial points driven home by Ian Cummins in this timely book, it seems to me that one of the most important for social workers in this second decade of the 21st century is about the centrality of individualism in neoliberal ideas. We need to resist the atomising and isolating effects of this, and at this later stage of reflection I can see that one of the key aspects of Boot Out Austerity was that it was a collective action. We walked together, talked together, sang together, thereby creating something that was far greater than the sum of its parts.

Taking to the streets in numbers made us visible, and this visibility and joining together was added to by our use of social media and by the meetings we held each evening. We were joined by service users, campaigners from groups such as Disabled People Against Cuts, social care workers, community workers and other concerned citizens. Since the walk I have learned how social workers from around the world were following our actions. Members of the professional social work associations in the Netherlands and Romania have told of how they were inspired by Boot Out Austerity, while a Canadian colleague gave the audience of a talk he was giving in Toronto the opportunity to follow our live streaming on Twitter.

So why did we take this action together? Our aims at the outset were to highlight the devastating impact that austerity is having on people who use social care and social work services, and to add our voices to those who are calling for an end to these policies. Again, it is only since we did the walk that other effects of it have become clear.

You will read in the pages that follow about the 'poverty paradox' of social work. Social workers work predominantly with people who are poor – those who are most affected by austerity – and yet there is a 'poverty-blindness' that affects many of us. There are probably many reasons for this, not least the insidious effects of neoliberalism in pushing social work away from a supporting function towards those of assessment, policing and care management and a preoccupation with risk. Furthermore, the individualising tendency of neoliberalism makes us see risk as coming from individuals – a child's parents for example – rather than from the poverty-inducing social structures that are all around us.

So a 'poverty-aware paradigm for social work practice' is needed, to inform a new attempt by social workers to engage with tackling poverty. We did not set out to make social workers more poverty-aware as one of our aims, but I know that we achieved this, at least in one case, as my own consciousness of modern-day poverty was very much raised. To give one particularly compelling example, to visit food banks and to speak with people running them brought home the iniquitous effects of benefit sanctions, which should have no place in a country as rich as ours.

With all the caveats that are rightly voiced about not living in a mythical golden social work past, it can still be said that we have known times when there was a more poverty-minded social work, and we can learn from and be encouraged by these times. I was heartened to discover that social workers were amongst the founders of the Child Poverty Action Group in the 1960s and that BASW had strong connections with it from its inception. Many years ago, BASW had a Special Interest Group on poverty, and I am pleased to say that out of Boot Out Austerity is emerging a BASW Austerity Action Group. In these pages, Ian Cummins poses a challenge to the leadership of the social work profession, which he claims, rightly in my view, has been disappointingly quiet about the impact of poverty on individuals and communities. The challenge for BASW and other social work organisations is to persist in putting and keeping poverty on the agenda and in facilitating and nurturing social workers' efforts to address it in their practices.

I welcome the emphasis here on the Professional Capabilities Framework and its potential for making anti-poverty social work a key requirement of professional development. Benefits advice and advocacy, income maximisation and debt counselling should all be seen as core social work business, as should community-based approaches. Social workers can take collective action too, and because we can, we have to.

When we set off on our walk, all the commentators and media pundits were predicting a landslide for Theresa May and the austerity-practising Conservative Party. As we now know, that did not happen. Since the publication of the Labour manifesto with its commitment to investment in public services, and the shock election result on 8 June, the political landscape has looked different. To be against austerity and for greater investment is becoming normalised and bordering on the mainstream. As Ian Cummins says, social attitudes can shift and have done so, for example with regard to race, gender and sexuality, and social work values have played a part in this. Social work values can help too in shifting views on poverty, austerity and the individuals and communities bearing the brunt of this. All of us in the social work community can play our part in this, whether by organising collective actions, addressing the material needs of individual service users, making alliances with service users and campaigning groups such as Disabled People Against Cuts, researching the impact of austerity, teaching students to be poverty-aware in their practice, or writing books that set out the social, political, economic and philosophical roots of neoliberalism and austerity and their alternatives.

Early on the seventh day of Boot Out Austerity we came across the Runcorn Old Bloom Library, a wooden cupboard standing in a public garden just off Runcorn High Street that is always open for people to put books in or take them away. We put in a copy of Mary O'Hara's *Austerity Bites* as a gift from the Boot Out Austerity walkers to the people of Runcorn. A week or so later I received an email from someone to tell me they had borrowed it. When we next arrange a march aimed at increasing poverty awareness, I will carry a copy of Ian Cummins' *Poverty, Inequality and Social Work* in my backpack, in order to pass it on as a vital part of our collective action.

Guy Shennan
Chair, British Association of Social Workers 2014-2018,
and Boot Out Austerity walker
1 August 2017

References

Fuller, S. (ed) (1991) *The Poetry of Protest*, London: BBC/Longman.

McGrath, L., Walker, C. and Jones, C. (2016) 'Psychologists Against Austerity: mobilising psychology for social change', *Critical and Radical Social Work*, vol 4, no 3, pp 409-13

O'Hara, M. (2015) *Austerity Bites: A journey to the sharp end of cuts in the UK*, Bristol: Policy Press.

Introduction

This work seeks to explore the impact of neoliberalism and austerity politics on the role of social work and wider welfare provision. Social work has to be analysed within a social, political and economic context, and 'political' is used here in its broadest sense. This work examines the social, political and cultural contexts, within which, social work has developed as a profession. It is impossible to understand fully current social policy and social work organisational structures without examining their roots. This exercise not only highlights the shifts that have taken place, but also the continuities. The structure of the book mirrors this. Chapter 1 looks at the development of neoliberal ideas. These have been the most dominant in economic and political thought since the election of Margaret Thatcher's first government in May 1979. Chapter 2 examines debates about the nature of class and inequality in the UK. It argues that these are of continuing importance to social work as a profession. The profession is committed to social justice but also the majority of social work takes place with marginalised groups. Chapter 3 uses the work of contemporary critical theorists including Imogen Tyler to analyse the nature of 'advanced marginality' and 'stigma'. It argues that neoliberalism has created economic conditions which serve to create spatially concentrated areas of poverty and disadvantage. These areas and their residents become stigmatised. Chapter 4 is an exploration of the welfare and penal systems during the period of neoliberalism. Chapter 5 explores contemporary social work practice in an era when inequality has become more deeply entrenched. Chapter 6 seeks to offer a new or revised model of a social state based on notions of equality, mutuality and reciprocity.

Chapter 1 considers the development of neoliberal ideas in a context of austerity. While the impact of neoliberal thinking on social policy is examined in more detail in subsequent chapters, some key themes are introduced in this chapter. One is that neoliberalism cannot be examined as a purely economic project, as the economics of neoliberalism is inextricably linked to shifts in social attitudes and cultural tropes – particularly the emphasis on individualism. These attitudes underpin a more punitive approach in social and penal policy. Indeed, Garland (2001) notes that the decline in the 'rehabilitative ideal' has profound implications, leading to social work practice that is increasingly focused on risk management, audit and bureaucratic responses, creating a tension between the expressed professional values of social work and the practice environment.

The book then goes on to explore the implications of these moves across a range of areas of social work practice. It argues that the profession has become enmeshed in policies or initiatives that are essentially punitive in their approaches. In social work there has always been a complex relationship between its controlling functions and an expressed commitment to emancipatory approaches. While acknowledging that there is a danger in romanticising a golden age of radical social work, the recent punitive shift must be challenged. I conclude in this chapter that current economic pressures on services, counter-intuitively, provide a possible route to a rediscovery of a relational approach to social work across all fields of practice.

This book is strongly influenced by opponents of the neoliberal project, in particular, Pierre Bourdieu and Loïc Wacquant. Their analysis of the impact of neoliberalism on the public provision of welfare is at the root of the theoretical framework that is applied to the development of policy. Wacquant argues that the shift in economic, welfare and social policy has led to the 'criminalisation of poverty'. This phrase captures both the legal reality of policies such as zero tolerance that criminalise homelessness and homeless people, and also the psychological impact – it becomes a crime to be poor. The architecture of these approaches is outlined in the chapters that explore poverty (Chapter 2), advanced marginality (Chapter 3) and the decline of the social state (Chapter 4). One of the key arguments put forward is that these changes are the direct result of cultural attitudes that neoliberalism has developed or strengthened.

The book sits very much in a tradition and approach that sees poverty and its associated social problems as the result of structural and economic issues. It is also very heavily influenced by the arguments of the late Stuart Hall that culture is important – although economics is important, it does not provide a complete analysis. As Wacquant (2009a, 2009b) demonstrates, neoliberal economic policies have had profound impacts on the social structures of urban communities. The existing networks of social capital have struggled to survive the changing patterns of work and employment, leading to a shift in the role of social work. In Bourdieu's famous analysis of the right and left hands of the state, where the right represents the forces of law and order, social work identifies itself with the left that represents welfare. As Garrett (2007) argues, however, there are dangers in this binary analysis, as it clearly fails to capture the dual or liminal nature of social work, which attempts or is asked to be both disciplinary and emancipatory at the same time.

Since 1979, neoliberalism has become the dominant political ideology. Developments in social policy have to be understood within this context. The key themes of neoliberalism – a reduced role for the state, the introduction of market mechanisms into the provision of public services, individualism and liberty as key political values – have profound implications for the functions and role of social work as a profession. They are reflected in new patterns of organisation or the provision of services, and also in cultural attitudes. The economic impact of neoliberalism, in particular, the rise in inequality, is examined in Chapter 5. However, its dominance is not limited to the economic or political sphere. The roots of a more punitive approach to social and welfare policy are firmly presented within the broader philosophy of Friedrich Hayek, Milton Friedman and the Chicago School and its successors (see Chapter 4).

Social work in the UK overwhelmingly takes place in poorer areas or with marginalised individuals, and the two groups clearly overlap. These issues are considered in more depth in Chapter 3. My thinking in this area is clearly influenced by Bourdieu, Wacquant and Savage's approach to modern social class and inequality.

In his discussion of the potentially marginalising impact of severe mental illness, Kelly (2005) uses the term 'structural violence' to describe the interaction between factors such as gender, race, poverty and class. This theoretical framework is used throughout this book to examine these issues. The huge economic and political changes that neoliberalism has influenced have created a more divided and segregated society – this book considers the broad implications of these trends. Wilkinson and Pickett (2009) demonstrate that inequality has social and psychological and not just economic impacts. There are vast differences between physical and mental health as well as the life chances of the richest and poorest in modern societies. These differences are greatest in the most unequal societies. Social work exists to mitigate these outcomes. Chapter 6 argues that the work of Martha Fineman, Emmanuel Levinas and Marian Barnes can be used as a basis for a development of a more relational approach to social work. Such an approach would reject the bureaucratic risk dominated paradigms that have, in my opinion, done so much harm, including those who work in social services and those who use the services provided.

The welfare state is a key character in this book. I am someone who has benefited enormously from educational opportunities, including the opportunity to attend one of the world's leading universities. I would not have been able to do so without state funding as well as the support of my family. The welfare state is often derided as monolithic, wasteful and dependency-producing. Part of the motivation for writing this work is to challenge those notions. Rather than being part of the problem, perhaps, just perhaps, social investment in health, education and social services might be part of the answer.

ONE

Social work in the era of neoliberalism and austerity

This chapter examines the key features of neoliberal thought. It then explores the links between these ideas and the development of social and welfare policies. The main argument advanced here is that the influence of neoliberal ideas has been a key factor in the increasingly punitive context of welfare. These underlying factors need to be understood as part of the analysis of trends in social welfare provision and also the changing relationship between services and service users.

Key features of neoliberal thought

In common with all political and economic ideologies, neoliberalism is a flexible term in that it covers a range of thinkers. There is a danger that such terms are used indiscriminately or as terms of abuse. For example, Labour critics of former Prime Minister Tony Blair label his economic and social policies as 'neoliberal'. In fact, certainly the first years of his premiership were far from the tenets of neoliberalism, as there was a very significant public investment in education, health and welfare provision (Toynbee and Walker, 2011). As another example the cover of David Harvey's (2005) Marxist analysis of neoliberalism has pictures of General Pinochet, military dictator in Chile, Ronald Reagan, Margaret Thatcher and Deng Xiaoping, testament to the reach and also the flexibility of neoliberal thought.

Stedman-Jones (2012) argues that the political and electoral success of parties committed to or influenced by neoliberal ideas means that there is a danger of seeing their rise as inevitable. In the UK context, this is certainly the narrative of Thatcherism that is presented by writers such as Sandbrook (2013) and Moore (2014). It should also be noted that it was a narrative that Thatcher – 'there is no alternative' (see Young, 2013) – was keen to emphasise. This ignores the real possibility that if there had been an election in the autumn of 1978, then James Callaghan and a Labour government would have been returned. The Thatcher government of 1979 marks a clear political shift, the ramifications of which are still being played in modern British politics. The post-war period was dominated by Keynesian economics and the development of a modern welfare state (Kynaston, 2007, 2008), which was an anathema to neoliberals. Keynesian economic policy was broadly followed in the UK by both Conservative and Labour parties. As Ken Loach's film 'The Spirit of 1945' captures, there was a post-war commitment not to return to the mass unemployment and social deprivation and division of the 1930s. Clement Attlee (see Bew, 2016), the unassuming former social worker, led a government that introduced reforms that were to shape British society for the next 40 years. These included the creation of the National Health Service and a commitment to full employment and education (Timmins, 1995). In this rather more optimistic period, the state, or at least the social state, was not generally viewed in such hostile terms as it later came to be by both Left and Right. The Left subsequently came to view the state as replicating and entrenching the inequalities and failings of capitalism – welfare was not progressive, but a means of disciplining the poor (Piven and Cloward, 2012). For the Right, the state came to be seen as too powerful, restricting individual liberty in the name of equality and inefficiently spending other people's money on incompetent bureaucrats. The period, from 1945 to 1976, of expansion of social welfare provision was very much a top-down process, with professionals such as doctors and teachers seen as the experts who were able to develop the appropriate services to meet the needs of the wider populace.

A strong school of thought always remained opposed to the development of the post-war, Keynesian welfare state. Stedman-Jones (2012, p 3) traces the development of modern neoliberal thought from the Freiburg School and the London School of Economics and Political Science's (LSE) response to the Great Depression. Hayek was most closely associated with the work of economists at the LSE in this period. The Freiburg School, later known as ordoliberals (after its journal *Ordo*), argued that the state had a key role to play in the maintenance of the market. This approach was in contrast to Roosevelt's New Deal, in which the public sector and public works had a key role to play in stimulating the economy (Leuchtenburg, 2009). Both the New Deal and the Freiburg School should be viewed as a response to the wider social and political pressures of the 1930s – mass unemployment, the growth of political extremism and the consequent spectre of totalitarianism. There was recognition within these approaches that a free market without some form of government intervention could potentially create the social conditions that would lead to huge political upheavals.

Hayek and the roots of neoliberalism

The most influential text in the modern development of neoliberal thought is Hayek's *The road to serfdom*, originally published in 1944. At the time it was written, it ran counter to most of the prevailing dominant economic and political ideas, as the demands of the wartime economy greatly expanded and strengthened the role of the state. Hayek and his followers were completely opposed to the extension of these ideas and roles into the post-war period, and the fundamentals of modern neoliberalism can all be found in Hayek's work.

Two key beliefs are at the heart of neoliberal ideas: the *supremacy of the market* (as the most effective means established for the distribution of resources), and a belief in *liberty* (defined here as freedom from state or other interference) as the supreme social and political value. Hayek argued that the role of the state should be to ensure that markets could operate – so, for example, a process for enforcing commercial contracts is needed, and personal and company taxation needs to be as low as possible, as this will increase incentives for individuals to work harder as they will receive greater rewards. It is also argued that low taxation rewards entrepreneurs and risk takers.

In 1947, Hayek organised a meeting at Mont Pelerin in Switzerland. Here, a group of economists and other intellectuals and academics met to plot the defence of liberalism against what they saw as the forces of collectivism. For the Mont Pelerin Society, as it came to be known, 'collectivism' was a very broad term that not only included fascist and communist totalitarian states, but also the emerging post-war social democracies of Europe. The Mont Pelerin Society became a key vehicle for the development and promulgation of neoliberal ideas. Hayek recognised that there was a need to influence the formation of policy, but that this was a slow, often circuitous, process. There was a key role for think-tanks – funded by sympathetic businessmen – and also for journalists and academics. One of the undoubted successes of neoliberalism has been the extent to which its key ideas – efficiency of the market, the bureaucratic and sclerotic nature of government bureaucracies and a belief that success is the result of individual hard work – have become so widely disseminated and deeply entrenched within popular discourse. From the 1970s onwards, think-tanks have had a key role to play in this process. For example, the Heritage Foundation and the Cato Institute in the US and the Centre for Policy in the UK have been notable for the role they have played. This amounts to an outsourcing of the development of government policy, bypassing Civil Service and government processes that are viewed as opposed to change.

In 1950, Hayek left the LSE and took up a post at the University of Chicago. From this point, the University of Chicago and its Department of Economics became the centre for the development and spread of neoliberal ideas. In the 1950s and early 1960s, neoliberal ideas were very much at the margins of political thought, and their influence on government policies of the time was very limited. In the US, Lyndon Johnson's 'Big Society' (Dallek, 2004) social welfare programmes were the sorts of government largesse that Mont Pelerin members opposed on philosophical and ethical grounds. In 1962 Milton Friedman published his most famous work, *Capitalism and freedom*. This was a sustained attack on the role of government – apart from its role in the maintenance of the rule of law. In Friedman's schema the market was the only means to successfully deliver social goods.

Hayek was a key influence in creating the intellectual shift that occurred, preparing the ground for the subsequent election success of Margaret Thatcher. While individualism is a key trope of all forms of liberalism, in neoliberalism, there is a zealous commitment to its pursuit. This can best be seen in the work of the libertarian Institute of Economic Affairs (IEA), a Right-wing think-tank that played a key role in the 1970s development of social and economic policy ideas. Following the election of Margaret Thatcher as Leader of the Conservative Party in 1975, the IEA became increasingly influential in the formation of policy. In part its role was to float ideas – often ones that might be seen as too extreme for the party leader to introduce. These would then make their way via sympathetic newspapers such as the *Daily Telegraph* into more mainstream debates. The IEA offered a series of market-based solutions in this period, and was also in the vanguard of attacks on the trade union movement.

The political successes of the Reagan and Thatcher administrations are usually regarded as ushering in a period where a belief in the efficacy of the free market became deeply embodied. Friedman's work, alongside others in the Chicago School such as Becker (1968), was heavily influenced by so-called Rational Choice Theory (RCT), which posits that individuals make rational choices using a cost-benefit model. Free markets allow individuals to make these decisions, and it is not for the state to interfere in the choices of consenting rational adults. Becker's work on crime is one way that the idea of free markets moved successfully from the economic to the broader social sphere. Both Thatcher and Reagan were elected on a platform that saw government as too big, unwieldy and expensive. The themes of their campaigns were very similar – a need to bring government spending under control, to cut personal taxation, reduce bureaucracy and tackle the power of the trade union movement. The post-war boom, from 1945 to the OPEC crisis of 1973 and subsequent inflation caused by a spike in the price of oil, had seen an expansion of the public sector to include social housing, major industries such as steel and coal and utilities including gas, electricity and telecommunications. In the UK, the Thatcher governments undertook a policy of privatisation whereby shares in major public utilities were sold to individual investors. The largest and most popular privatisation electorally was the sale of council housing (under the Right to Buy).

Neoliberalism is not simply concerned with, as its proponents would see it, the more efficient operation of the free market. It also seeks to expand markets or extend market forces to areas of the economy or social provision previously considered as standing outside of it. This is a mixture of libertarian objections to the state having a role in these areas (Nozick, 1974) and economic ones. In addition, public providers of, for example, health and education, were seen by neoliberals as being dominated by provider interests, inefficient bureaucracies and the interests of public sector trade unions. Neoliberalism argues that the discipline of the market and competition is required to tackle these issues. The mantra of choice is a powerful feature of many neoliberal approaches. Friedman, for example, was a long-time supporter of a school voucher scheme that he felt would improve choices for parents who would be able to move their children from under-performing schools. It is one of the reasons that their ideas have become so popular as most of us see choice and the right to exercise it as positive. In the recent debates in England about the proposals to allow the return of grammar schools, for example, supporters of the policy presented parental choice as a key factor although this policy is not now going ahead.

Individualism – a belief that states and institutions should not restrict the choices and freedom of citizens is one of the key tropes of neoliberalism. This may help explain some of its enduring power and success in the US and UK, where there are strong cultural and historical attachments to such notions. The concept of individualism raises important questions for professions such as social work that are explicitly concerned with notions of social justice. As a result, social work often finds itself at odds with the prevailing *zeitgeist* – although it should be said that the profession often struggles or fails to acknowledge this. Individualism is based on the largely mythical figure of the self-made man (or very occasionally woman). Since the 1980s, the development of celebrity culture alongside a much greater emphasis on the self means that broader structural and other issues have been marginalised. Fraser (2013a) argues that the language of radical identity and feminist politics of the 1960s has been successfully colonised by neoliberalism so that such issues are recast as issues of individualism. For neoliberalism, inequality is a fact of human life – put simply, we are not equal – not in terms of the law or civic rights, but in terms of skills and abilities. Any attempts to overcome inequality are to be opposed because they are doomed to fail as a result of this basic fact. In addition, any state attempts to tackle inequality will involve higher taxation – a restriction on liberty itself or state-imposed restrictions on choice a further dilution of the liberty of the subject.

The neoliberal model of low personal taxation, the expansion of the market into areas such as health and education, the privatisation of large state assets and the reduction in power of organised labour is one that has been exported from Chicago around the world. Stedman-Jones (2012, p 8) notes that these key tenets were accepted and adopted by policy-makers of leading global institutions such as the International Monetary Fund (IMF), The World Bank and European Union (EU).

Social work and other areas of welfare have clearly been affected by the expansion of the market, although there have always been private providers of services in these areas. For example, Scull's (2015) history of madness shows that there has always been the option of private provision for wealthier members of society. The National Health Service and Community Care Act 1990 explicitly created a market in residential and other community services for adults with mental health, learning disabilities or other health needs. The majority of adult residential caring or support for people to remain living independently in their own homes is now provided by commercial enterprises. As well as providing an example of the expansion of the market into new areas, the care sector highlights changes in employment. The conditions of employment are such that many workers are on zero-hours contracts and do not get paid travelling time. This model of employment – precarious employment (see Standing, 2011) – has become increasingly common whereby in the name of flexibility, employees enjoy few, if any, meaningful rights, and have no guarantee of continued employment. The contrast with the regular, unionised patterns of work that characterised Fordism could not be greater.

The work of key thinkers such as Hayek, Friedman and Becker was premised on the assumption that individualism is the key driving force in social, economic and political development. Mrs Thatcher's famous remark that "there is no such thing as society, only individuals and families", captures the essence of this. The market is not only seen as the most effective means of allocation of resources; it is also the most accurate reflection of human nature. In this view, life is competitive and skills are not distributed evenly among citizens. The market decides on the monetary value of those skills, and pay and other benefits should reflect this. Following the classic laws of supply and demand, a higher price is placed on skills that are in short or limited supply. It is also suggested that economic freedoms bring with them political and civil freedoms. In this schema, political liberalism and modern democracy is an outcome of capitalism. The extension of constitutional and legal rights is linked to the individualism and demands for market freedoms that accompany the rise of the influence of the bourgeoisie. In this model, the separation of economic and political powers creates two counterbalancing spheres of influence.

The neoliberal conception of the state is most clearly enunciated in Nozick's (1974) *Anarchy, state and utopia*. In this schema, the state should act as a 'nightwatchman' for wider society. The role is to ensure that law and order is maintained, but any other state interventions are viewed as either a restriction on individual liberty or interference in the workings of the market, or a combination of the two. Hayek's (1944) *The road to serfdom* is not just a warning against the totalitarian regimes of Nazi Germany and the Soviet Union; it is also a critique of social democratic welfare regimes. For Hayek, these regimes have the potential to overrule individual choices of the free market. It is acknowledged that the free market may not be perfect in this regard, but it can reflect individual choices in a way that government bureaucracy never can.

The Chicago School of economists placed notions of 'choice' at the centre of economic and by extension, political, life. In this area, Becker's (1968) work is key. It is a radical recasting of the notion of the social. He argued that all human behaviour could be understood using economic approaches because it is essentially about deciding how to allocate available resources to which ends. Becker, famously, saw the decision to commit a crime as a cost-benefit analysis undertaken by the offender. This process involved considering factors such as the likelihood of being detected, the potential punishment and the rewards of the crime. This, of course, assumes that all offenders act rationally when committing a crime, and seems to discount a number of other factors that might influence their behaviour – most notably, the impact of alcohol and drugs.

The notions of choice and individualism are clearly inextricably linked. They are at the root of the neoliberal attack on the welfare state (explored in more detail below in Chapter 4). However, it is important that these ideas are introduced here, as they are key to understanding developments in social and welfare policies in the past 30 years. They also help to explain the shifting political attitudes to the role of social work.

Thinkers on the Right are wary of the welfare state for economic and social reasons. As outlined above, the welfare state can only be funded by taxation either on corporations or on individuals. Either route distorts the markets, acts as a drain on individual initiative and entrepreneurship, and is wasteful. In this schema, government or public bodies are inherently inefficient because they stand outside of the discipline that market competition creates. State bureaucracy will inevitably include regulation, and in the Right's terms, 'burdens on business', be this health and safety regulations or employees' rights. In addition, public officials are portrayed as lazy, time-servers waiting for an early retirement and the benefits of a generous pension. The statutory social work profession is thus part of a state bureaucracy, but also, as outlined below, it is part of the processes of the welfare state that at best creates dependency or at worst indulges or excuses anti-social behaviour. Neoliberalism is not opposed to charity or philanthropy – how people choose to spend their money is a matter of choice. Neoliberals object to this becoming a state-run activity.

The criticisms of the post-war welfare state were not limited to thinkers on the Right. The late 1960s and early 1970s saw the development of a number of radical critiques of welfarism. Writers focusing on the health and education systems came to see them not as sites for potential positive social investment, but more as areas that replicated or buttressed the inequalities of late modern capitalism. Illich (2003), for example, saw the modern health service as a vehicle for the exploitation of the sick by 'Big Pharma'. The second wave of feminism was implicitly critical of a whole range of social and political institutions that reproduced broader gender inequalities (see Oakley, 2005). Alongside this, the New Left produced a radical critique of social democratic capitalism, highlighting issues such as race and policing (Hall et al, 2014). Willis (2000), in *Learning to labour*, explored the ways in which selective education replicated the clear class and social stratification of British industry of that time. The realist drama and novels of the late 1950s and early 1960s are replete with disaffected angry young men (they are almost always men) such as Joe Lampton in John Braine's 1957 *Room at the top*, Arthur Seaton in Alan Sillitoe's 1958 *Saturday night and Sunday morning* and Vic Brown in Stan Barstow's 1960 *A kind of loving*. They see Britain as a claustrophobic, class-bound society that stifles individualism, creativity and ambition, themes that originate on the Left, but were then taken up by the Right, and a journey that many writers of the period, for example Amis and Osborne, took themselves. For the Left in this period, social work, for example, in Ken Loach's searing 'Cathy Come Home' is an adjunct to a heartless, uncaring state. In the classic TV drama, social workers are portrayed as indifferent at best or cruel and almost sadistic, as they remove Cathy's children.

In addition to the impact on the functioning of the market, the Right argues that the welfare state creates dependency. Put simply, this view is that individuals do not have to work as they can rely on generous state benefits. The discourse of the moral failings of the poor has a long and undistinguished history (Welshman, 2013) that will be explored in more depth in later chapters. In this context, it is most closely associated with Murray (1990) and the term 'the underclass'. Murray, incidentally, heavily supported and given publicity by the IEA, argued that the welfare state had created a new class, the underclass. For Murray, this group is cut off from the broad economic and moral development of wider society. Welfare rewards rather than punishes such individuals for their poor behaviour and choices. Interestingly, for Murray and others, welfare professionals such as social workers, with their commitment to 'woolly ideas' such as social justice, are often seen as part of this process.

These views were given political expression by the former Secretary of State for Education, Michael Gove, in a speech in November 2013. He indicated that too many social workers had been on degree courses that were dominated by "idealistic" Left-wing dogma that allows people from troubled backgrounds to "make excuses". He went on to suggest that social workers concentrated on obtaining benefits for service users rather than "helping them to change their own approach to life" (Gove, 2013) He did soften the attack somewhat by acknowledging the demands on front-line social workers. As, indeed, had David Cameron at the Conservative Party conference that year, when he called social work a "noble" profession. However, the reports of his speech focused almost entirely on the criticisms that play on and reinforce deeply held stereotypes of the profession.

The state and neoliberalism

Questions about the nature and role of the state are fundamental to any discussion of political theory. The key thinkers in the development of neoliberalism saw the state as inefficient, bloated, interventionist and creating dependency. And it was felt that in an increasingly globalised world, the role for state intervention in the market was increasingly diminished. There is a danger of overstating the case here, as clearly powerful companies or individuals have always had significant political influence. However, the power of huge multinationals and global players such as Google, Samsung and Amazon is a political reality that modern governments have to face, and the Thatcher and Reagan governments were at the forefront of these reforms to state structures. The aim of neoliberalism was twofold – to reduce the size of the state (apart from the functions of law and order; see Chapter 4 on the penal state), and also to introduce market mechanisms wherever possible. A smaller state would be welcome on both philosophical and also economic grounds, meaning that individuals have more choice, but it also costs less, so rates of personal taxation could be reduced, particularly for higher earners.

One of the strengths of neoliberalism has been the way that it has come to define the terms of the debate in economic, cultural and political spheres. Giroux (2011) argues that neoliberalism has pushed out other ideas. Neoliberalism thus becomes a political project not simply an economic one. The accommodation that parties of the Left made with some of the key tenets of neoliberalism is most evident in debates about the role of the state. From very different perspectives, both the radical Right and Left are wary of state intervention, seeing it as either a destroyer of individual freedom or a protector of vested interests and a barrier to radical social progress. Interestingly, both perspectives are critical of the social work profession for its role in these processes. From the 1980s onwards, governments of both the Right and Left have taken an approach that sees the state as an equal player – or, in the jargon, a 'stakeholder' – alongside others. The state is seen as an enabler or creator of public/private partnerships.

One way of conceptualising this political (re)birth of neoliberalism is to see it as a reaction against the statism of the 1960s and 1970s. From this perspective, the state had taken on too great a role, not only in terms of the economy – nationalised industries and regulation – but also in the daily lives of citizens. And this is where the social and economic come together. The collapse of the Heath government in 1974 following the Miners' Strike was seared into the brains of Thatcher and her advisers, who were determined to reduce the power of the trade union movement (Gilmour, 1992).

In Skelcher's (2000) conceptualisation of the state, three models are identified: the overloaded state of the 1960s/1970s; the hollowed-out state of the 1980s/early 1990s; and the congested state of the late 1990s. The process of transition from the 'overloaded' state of the 1970s involved the privatisation of state assets and a new wave of trade union legislation that restricted the rights of members. Hayek (1944) was strongly opposed to all forms of collectivism. In this model of the overloaded state, trade unions were seen as restricting individual freedom and also as distorting the market. Policies such as the reduction in the role and powers of trade unions were made in the name of market 'flexibility'. Flexibility is an example of what Wacquant (2009a) terms 'doxa', where *doxa* derives from the Greek, and means 'a commonly held belief'. Wacquant uses doxa to mean terms that set or make the parameters of debate or what is sayable or thinkable. Flexibility, choice, individualism – the doxa of neoliberalism – are very powerful, reflecting not only the political success of the parties of the Right, but also the difficulty of shifting the terms of the debate. Who can possibly be opposed to choice? This obscures the fact that choice in free markets is a function of resources and power – it is simply impossible for everyone to exercise choice, as resources are not infinite. One example illustrates this point. Supporters of selective education in the UK emphasise that this is a matter of parental choice, but this ignores two important facts – schools choose pupils by means of an examination, and there is a limit on places.

It is important to recognise that there is a gap between theoretical and economic models and the reality of day-to-day politics and government. For example, the first Thatcher government from 1979 onwards was committed to cutting public expenditure. However, the huge rise in unemployment meant that public spending increased (Gilmour, 1992). The ideological shift in attitudes to the role of the state was well established in the early 1980s; the strategy of influencing the media and policy via public intellectuals and think-tanks that had been initiated at Mont Perelin (see Mirowski and Piehwe, 2015) also bore fruit in this period. At the same time, the socioeconomic changes that followed the oil crisis of the early 1970s had a profound influence. The decline in manufacturing industries – mining, steel production and shipbuilding – meant that union membership subsequently declined, as the rise of finance and service sectors, and with it the casualisation of employment (more part-time and short-term contract work) made it more difficult for unions to recruit and organise members. There was also a significant shift in the role of women in the workforce. These factors combine to produce huge changes in the political and economic life of the country. The number of trade union members dropped significantly as did the influence of the movement. The largest trade unions were to be found in the public sector.

While neoliberalism sought to limit the role of the state in economic and social matters, the demands of late modern capitalism actually meant that a role was required for the state. In certain areas, for example, education, the state has a key role to play, as late modern capitalism requires an increasingly well-educated workforce. So for Blair's New Labour, expanding higher education and increasing the number of graduates was key to modernising the British economy, although it should be recognised that this is not the whole workforce – there are increasingly complex social and class divisions within modern Britain (see Savage, 2015), and educational achievement is one of the key determinants of individual position within these structures. (These issues are explored in more depth in Chapter 2, which examines the nature of modern poverty.) The free market has never been able to ensure that the whole population receives an education – to achieve this the state has had to intervene.

The shift that occurred in the 1980s/90s, that Skelcher termed the 'hollowing out' of the state, saw a new set of arrangements for governance established, including a new range of regulators and inspection regimes for public bodies, such as Ofsted for schools and eventually children's services. Pollitt and Bouckaert (1999) outline this development of 'new public management' (NPM). NPM was an attempt to introduce some elements of the market, such as competition, to public services. In this model, it was important that there was a purchaser/provider split to break up perceived monopolies. In the social care field, this was enshrined in the NHS and Community Care Act 1990, which introduced significant changes to the structure, provision and arrangements for the delivery of services. Policies were written in the language of consumer choice. The shift in the language of social work – client, customer, service user or expert by experience – reflects this dynamic. These shifts also illustrate the tension underpinning the wider social work role. None of the terms are completely successful in capturing the potential complexities inherent in the relationship between social workers and individuals who come into contact with services. NPM led to the development of an audit culture, so that in health, education and other areas, an organisation's performance was measured against a series of Key Performance Indicators (KPIs), which for many was seen as an attack on their professional independence and autonomy. And it also created a huge bureaucratic structure to manage the data.

The political dominance of parties of the Right in the 1980s and early 1990s forced progressive parties to make accommodations. The US and UK administrations of Clinton and Blair are both examples of this, but similar approaches were followed by the Hawke and Keating administrations in Australia, for example. For Blair, the old politics of Right and Left – free market versus state intervention – was dead. He did not explicitly state this, but the market-orientated approaches had won. For progressive parties to be electable, they would have to appeal to the 'aspirational' – such terms eventually become lost in a fog of doublespeak. However, at the start of the New Labour project, it was clear that Blair had successfully constructed a new progressive coalition of urban elites and more traditional Labour voters. He was skilfully able to appeal to the social liberal while also adopting recognisably social democratic policies with a focus on investment in public services. This was given intellectual gloss and termed the 'Third Way' by Giddens (1998) (that is, not free market capitalism and not 1970s statism). This recasting of social democracy saw the roots of progressive values in communitarianism rather than economic equality, and brought about a common ownership of the means of production.

Etzioni's (1993) work played a key role here. Communitarianism appeals to very traditional notions, seeing the development of community-orientated values as rooted in the key social institutions of the family, education and voluntary groups. This approach accepts that there is a role for community organisations – not necessarily, and preferably not, the state – to assist citizens who have fallen on hard times. However, it is wary of the dangers of 'rewarding' poor behaviour or encouraging dependency. The traditional Labour/social democratic concern with equality is replaced by a concern for equality of opportunity. This is not mere sophism; it is a reflection of a fundamental shift in thinking. Communitarianism has within it the roots of the more punitive approaches to social policy that characterised much of the later New Labour project (Butler and Drakeford, 2001).

The internal moves and shifts in politics in the UK that saw the demise of the Thatcher and Major governments followed by the New Labour administrations took place at a time of 'globalisation'. Globalisation is one of those terms that has become used so frequently that it almost loses any meaning. I use it here to refer to the process of trade liberalisation that occurred in the early 1980s that eventually resulted in the modern world market, dominated by huge corporations such as Apple, Samsung and Walmart. In these processes of the establishment of a world market, national and local governments have lost influence and the ability to counteract these trends. And the period prior to the 2008 banking crisis was one where the power and influence of neoliberal ideas were at their height.

Meritocracy

There has been something of a disconnect between the alleged rugged individualism of neoliberalism and a public policy discourse that commits itself to widening opportunity. This rhetoric has reached new heights post-Brexit, as Prime Minister Theresa May has sought to recast the Conservative Party as one that would seek to 'fight against the burning injustices' of poverty, race, class and health, and give people back 'control' of their lives (Swinford, 2016). She also stated that her administration would not 'entrench the advantages of the privileged few.' This was partly an internal political move to distance herself from the Cameron Cabinet, as she followed up this speech by dismissing Cameron's closest political ally, George Osborne. However, it also emphasised that the language of class – in this case, the denial of its existence – remains a key factor in modern British politics. Class is hiding in plain sight in political discourse. One of the features of these processes is that populist attacks on elites are led from within, May and her Cabinet being a prime example.

Littler (2013) highlights the fact that the rhetoric of meritocracy is universal – politicians from both the Left and Right of the political spectrum are allegedly committed to meritocratic ideals. As she notes, the overwhelming majority of those who use the term assume that it has a positive, progressive and anti-elitist meaning. It is used as a contrast to a hierarchical, class-bound society where opportunities are restricted by the luck of birth, and it appears to have particular resonance in the world of education. Thus the modern use of the term ignores its actual roots. Michael Young (2004) coined the term as a warning and a satirical comment on a society where elites were able to maintain their position while publicly committing themselves to a more egalitarian society. The current irony is that many features of Young's dystopian meritocratic society exist, but are held up as positives rather than negatives. Littler (2016, np) argues that the idea of meritocracy is thus 'currently being actively mobilised by members of a plutocracy to extend their own interests and power.' In Littler's phrase, meritocracy is part of a process that serves to marketise the very idea of equality. Meritocracy is thus not in opposition to the key themes of neoliberalism. As one of the key aspects of neoliberalism, highlighted by Foucault (2008), is that markets have to be produced, the overall effect of the rhetoric of meritocracy is to reproduce and entrench rather than to challenge class inequalities.

The strength of the notion of meritocracy is demonstrated by the fact that it is used so widely, and also that its core notions are hardly, if ever, challenged. Young (2001) expressed his frustration with the fact that warnings from his 1958 essay, 'The rise of meritocracy' (Young, 1958), had not been heeded. In both this 2001 piece and his original book, Young emphasised that education would have a key role in the creation of a meritocratic society. In describing the way that his satirical essay, denuded of its satirical content, had been taken up by politicians, he pointed out that:

> With an amazing battery of certificates and degrees at its disposal, education has put its seal of approval on a minority, and its seal of disapproval on the many who fail to shine from the time they are relegated to the bottom streams at the age of seven or before. (Young, 2001)

He argued that the impact on those who are deemed 'not to have merit' is completely overlooked by those enthusiastically committed to meritocracy. Its supporters simply fail to acknowledge that by definition, meritocracy becomes exclusionary rather than inclusive. As access to education expands, a new market or currency develops so that certain universities have great prestige. In the UK, the Russell Group of Universities – 'research-intensive, world-class universities' – form an elite grouping whose graduates go on to dominate professions such as medicine, law, journalism and banking (Savage, 2015).

Littler (2013) outlines the key assumptions that underpin the notion of meritocracy and the implications of a commitment to it. The first assumption is that intelligence, ability and talent is innate. The role of education systems is to identify those with ability, and ensure that this group can fulfil its potential, which is an implicit acceptance of a hierarchical and unequal society. Social mobility in this schema is always an individualised process – it is about working-class children 'escaping' the allegedly toxic environments – family, friends and neighbourhoods – where they were born to become members of the middle class. This is ultimately not an expression of a sense of community or reciprocal values; rather, it is a corrosive ethic of self-interest presented as a social good. The success of a few working-class children is used as a screen to mask the huge inequalities in broader society. Young (2001) contrasts the first Blair Cabinet, made up of Oxbridge-educated professional politicians, with Attlee's 1945 Cabinet that founded the modern welfare state. Attlee's Foreign Secretary was Ernest Bevin who left school at 11 and had a series of labouring jobs before his rise in the trade union movement. There are also modern examples of politicians such as Alan Johnson, who have not followed the Oxbridge, special adviser,

MP route to Cabinet, but they are increasingly rare, and ironically, this seems to be a particular issue for the Labour Party.

A fundamental objection to meritocracy is that it is dishonest and misleading. The logical outcome of social policies based on the rhetoric of meritocracy is not greater opportunities, but the hardening and reinforcing of social inequality. A meritocracy assumes that society is inevitably hierarchical – this means that as well as an elite, there must be a marginalised class. And education plays an increasing role in these processes. Young (2001, np) notes that the meritocratic elites become a new class, one that 'has the means at hand, and largely under its control, by which it reproduces itself.'

Austerity and the recasting of the welfare state

The banking crisis of 2008 led to the Brown Labour government in the UK bailing out the sector. The irony of government intervention and funds coming to the rescue of the loudest proponents of free market, anti-statist ideas was not lost on many. The banking crisis and the Eurozone debt crisis led to the introduction of a range of policies that came to be known as 'austerity'. As these measures were introduced by the Brown administration, Brown has become a much-derided figure; it is now rather forgotten that he received wide praise for his handling of the crisis. The bailout cost an estimated £141 billion (Oxfam, 2013). Austerity measures that were introduced by the coalition government from 2010 are presented as a necessary response to the state of the public finances after the bailout. It is overlooked that the Brown administration, at the same time as bailing out the banks, followed standard Keynesian principles and attempted to stimulate demand in the economy – for example, by reducing VAT and increasing capital spending on schools and social housing. In the period 2008-10, the poorest fifth of the population saw incomes grow at a rate of 3.4 per cent, while it was slowest for the richest two-fifths of the population, growing at a rate of 0.3 per cent (Oxfam, 2013, np).

Krugman (2015) describes austerity as a kind of fever that has infected elites across Western governments, and the coalition government in the UK was the one that was most infected. Austerity marks a huge departure from a Keynesian approach to economic management. Keynes argued that the lesson of the 1930s slump was the time for a fiscal stimulus – austerity should be introduced during a boom. When the coalition government was elected, they were able to present the introduction of austerity measures as what was required in a time of national emergency, using the Eurozone crisis and the situation in

Greece as constant reference points. Soon after taking office, David Cameron (2010, np) stated, 'Greece stands as a warning of what happens to countries that lose their credibility, or whose governments pretend that difficult decisions can somehow be avoided.' The use of Greece as a warning is important as the crisis in Greek government finances was consistently portrayed as being the result of an over-generous welfare state rather than as a result of the behaviour of elites. As Krugman concludes, the real purpose of austerity was not economic; it was political. The aim was to shrink the state and reduce social welfare provision, not just in response to the current crisis, but permanently.

The coalition introduced a range of austerity measures that in total amounted to the biggest cuts in state spending since the Second World War (Crawford, 2010). The Institute for Fiscal Studies (IFS) (2012) has calculated that there will be over 900,000 public sector jobs lost in the period 2011–18. The IFS found that the effect of the tax and benefit changes will increase absolute and relative poverty. Austerity has led to a period of economic stagnation combined with falling incomes and rising costs of living, meaning that many are struggling to manage. The coalition made the very significant decision to link increases in social security to the Consumer Price Index (CPI) rather than the Retail Price Index (RPI). As the RPI is higher, this means that benefits will become worth less. These changes have the greatest impact on the poorest members of society as basic costs such as food, housing and energy have all increased at rates higher than inflation over the last few years.

There has also been a shift in the nature of poverty over the past decade, with more younger people poor, and a rise in in-work poverty. The coalition removed the Education Maintenance Allowance (EMA) in England, which had paid £30 a week to those 16- to 19-year-olds from the poorest backgrounds who were in full-time education. The coalition also trebled tuition fees to £9,000 per annum; many universities will increase fees to £9,250 from 2017/18. Austerity policies also saw increases in Jobseeker's Allowance, Housing Benefit and Child Benefit being limited to 1 per cent for three years. One of the founding principles of welfare states, universalism (which creates social solidarity), is generally more efficient to administer and removes means testing. The taxing of Child Benefit for higher earners is an opening shot in undermining this principle. Galbraith (1964) noted that social insurance systems would be fatally undermined when the rich were able to buy themselves out of public provision. Why support taxes for services that you or your family will not use or consider inferior? This is increasingly the case in education and healthcare.

It is a statement of the obvious that these measures have a much greater impact on the poorest and most marginalised members of our society. Austerity was presented as a policy response to a national emergency, and, as we have seen, there are disputes about its extent and nature. Austerity is not the technocratic exercise in economic management that its supporters claim. It is an ideological attack on the foundations of the social contract that formed the basis of the post-war society. It is a second wave following the initial thrust of Thatcherism, and has real consequences for real people. Furthermore, cuts in the public sector have a double impact on women – not only are women more likely to use public services; they are also more likely to work in the public sector. Austerity will therefore have long-term consequences for gender equality and child poverty in the UK.

While the coalition government presented austerity as an emergency policy, it is clear that the changes to benefits and the more punitive regime of sanctions that have been introduced is part of a wider ideological attack on welfare generally. Garrett (2015) traces the use of the term 'welfare'. He demonstrates that it has developed overwhelmingly negative connotations, becoming shorthand for notions of dependency or exploitation of the system. For example, in the Conservative Party's *Responsibility Agenda* (Conservative Party, 2008, p 12), it was stated that 'ending Britain's welfare culture is a moral duty for any progressive government.' This statement, as well as giving the lie to any notion that austerity was forced on the coalition by economic circumstances, assumes that there is a welfare culture. It also seems to imply that a progressive government can be Conservative. Throughout his speeches, Cameron used the language of social justice – reform, fairness, modernising and progressive – to discuss these welfare policies.

I use two examples here to illustrate the impact of changes on welfare – the 'Bedroom Tax' and benefit sanctions.

The 'Bedroom Tax' was introduced in April 2013 in England. Changes that were introduced to Housing Benefit meant that the rent paid was reduced for what was termed 'under-occupancy', meaning that if a tenant was deemed to have one spare bedroom, they lost 14 per cent of their rent allowance. In the run-up to its introduction its supporters argued that the 'Bedroom Tax' would be fairer – it would ensure that social housing would be more equitably allocated – and it would also reduce expenditure. The 'Bedroom Tax' was based on the notion that there was a large group of families exploiting the Housing Benefit system to live in large houses at the public's expense, and it was argued that the policy would make them move to smaller properties. In reality, there were no smaller properties for families to rent. And the greatest objection to the tax was that it amounted to an attack on those most in need – people with disabilities or those caring for children with complex needs. Indeed, the government lost a case in the Supreme Court brought by two families. Jacqueline Carmichael, who is disabled and cannot share a room with her husband, had been subject to the tax, as had Paul and Susan Rutherford, who care for their severely disabled grandson, Warren, age 17, in a specially adapted three-bedroom bungalow. Rosa Curling, a solicitor at the law firm Leigh Day, who represented the Carmichaels, said:

> This is an extremely important and welcome decision which recognises that the government cannot trample over people's rights in the name of austerity.
> Our clients had a very clear medical need for two bedrooms and it's disappointing that the government chose to fight this case for three years, putting our clients through a long period of uncertainty. Our clients are delighted that justice has been done and they can now start to move on with their lives knowing that their rights as a disabled person and their right to a family life together will be respected. (quoted in Bowcott and Butler, 2016)

Ken Loach's film, 'I, Daniel Blake', won the Palme d'Or at the 2016 Cannes Film Festival and the Prix du Public at the 2016 Locarno International Film Festival. It has received widespread critical acclaim for its portrayal of the impact of austerity. The film tells the story of Blake, a 59-year-old joiner working in Newcastle. He has a heart attack and is unable to work. Those claiming Employment and Support Allowance (ESA) have to undergo a work capability assessment (WCA). Blake is then deemed fit for work despite the medical evidence. He attempts to appeal but finds the system almost impossible to negotiate. He befriends a young woman, Kate, who has been moved to Newcastle because of the new cap on Housing Benefit. The film portrays a harsh punitive bureaucracy that ignores basic needs – such as shelter and food. Loach's film is a dramatic portrayal of the impact of these measures on the most marginalised. It is also a film that shows that individuals in these circumstances resist and are not passive in the face of the difficulties and indifference that they face.

Loach's film is a dramatisation of the system of sanctioning introduced by the Jobseeker's Act 2013. The idea that the welfare state is over-generous – a 'soft touch', or an example of the 'something for nothing' society – has been a recurring theme in anti-welfare discourse. The sanctioning system was the subject of an independent review by Oakley that was presented to Parliament in 2014. Oakley began by outlining the case for sanctions:

> Benefit sanctions provide a vital backstop in the social security system for jobseekers. They ensure that, in return for the support provided by the state, claimants are held accountable for doing all they can to take on that support and to move back into work. This is a key element of the mutual obligation that underpins both the effectiveness and fairness of the social security system. (Oakley, 2014, p 9)

From this point on, the report is an indictment of the system, and particularly the way that claimants are kept informed whilst decisions are being made about the status of their claim and whether they will be sanctioned.

If an individual makes a claim for any of the following – Universal Credit, Income Support, Jobseeker's Allowance or ESA – they also sign a document that sets out their responsibilities, for example, applying for a certain number of jobs each week. If they fail to meet these conditions, they can have sanctions applied, that is, their benefits may be stopped. The most common reasons for having benefits sanctioned are: not doing enough to look for work, not turning up to a meeting at the Jobcentre, or not taking part in an employment or training scheme. The decision to sanction is not made by the personal advisers in Jobcentre Plus, but is referred to an independent decision-maker. Sanctions should not apply when the individual can demonstrate a 'good reason' for failing to meet the conditions, and these would include personal circumstances or bereavement. The Oakley Review found that not only were there poor levels of understanding among claimants of the requirements, but also of the sanctioning processes, including the right to appeal. Oakley notes that the complexity of the system and the range of personal circumstances meant that a number of claimants were actually unaware of what their usual rate of benefit payment should be. As a result, they found it difficult to know if a sanction had been applied and if so, what the amount was. Oakley also highlights that communication between staff and claimants around this issue was poor, citing examples of claimants receiving poorly drafted and confusing letters.

The impact of sanctions on individuals is clear. This group of people are less likely to have savings or resources to draw on – certainly for any prolonged period. Chapter 3, that discusses the impact of stigma, highlights the way that these issues atomise society and isolate individuals. One of the most obvious examples of the impact of changes in the benefits system – including the Housing Benefit cap and sanctions – has been the rise in the use of food banks. The Trussell Trust is a charity that coordinates food banks in the UK. In 2009-10, Trussell Trust food banks were operating in 29 local authorities across the UK; in 2013-14, there were food banks in 251 local authorities. Loopstra et al (2015, p 2), in their analysis of the extension of the use of food bank use, conclude that:

> More food banks are opening in areas experiencing greater cuts in spending on local services and central welfare benefits and higher unemployment rates. The rise in food bank use is also concentrated in communities where more people are experiencing benefit sanctions. Food parcel distribution is higher in areas where food banks are more common and better established, but our data also show that the local authorities with greater rates of sanctions and austerity are experiencing greater rates of people seeking emergency food assistance.

One of the leading critics of austerity, Professor Mark Blyth, sums it up thus:

> … the deliberate deflation of domestic wages and prices through cuts to public spending. (2013a, p 41)

The central aim of the policy is to reduce the state's debts and broader public spending so as to increase business confidence and investment. The reduction in state debt, it is argued, will also improve consumer confidence, leading to increased spending and economic growth. For example, in response to the Eurozone sovereign debt crisis, austerity policies were imposed on Greece. The imposition of these policies was based on a clear link being made between the fiscal crisis and an allegedly overgenerous social state. The same was to happen in the UK. Following the 2010 election in the UK, a coalition Liberal Democrat and Conservative government was formed. The Cameron administration, with his chief political ally, George Osborne as Chancellor, introduced a series of austerity measures that, they argued, were required as a response to an emergency in the national finances. The policies introduced followed almost classic neoliberal arguments – cuts in higher rate personal tax to encourage entrepreneurial activity and cuts in welfare spending to tackle the problems of welfare dependency.

Blyth (2013a) notes that austerity, although presented as an emergency solution to a national and international crisis, is actually a modern variant of well-established monetarist approaches. His attack on the policy is not just based on the economic arguments but is also couched in terms of social justice that should appeal to all social workers. (The full impact of austerity is discussed in detail in Chapter 2, which explores the nature of poverty and inequality in modern Britain.) Blyth notes that one of the attractions of austerity is the simplicity of its core claim – that the problem of debt cannot be solved with more debt. In her successful election campaigns, Mrs Thatcher portrayed herself as a prudent housewife running the nation's finances in the same way as she would the family budget. This is a comparison that was very powerful but actually fell apart at first analysis. Mrs Thatcher was married to a millionaire businessman, and national budgets cannot be reduced to a simple income/expenditure in the way that she suggested. Blyth argues that austerity does not have the same impact across society. The poorest lose out more because they are more reliant on public services and have little in the way of personal savings and so on to fall back on. Blyth sums his argument up as follows:

> Trying to get the lower end of the income distribution to pay the price of austerity through cuts in public spending is both cruel and mathematically difficult. Those who can pay won't, while those who can't pay are being asked to do so. (2013a, p 44)

In international terms, if all states reduce their spending at once – as happened in the Eurozone – then there is a lack of the necessary spending required for growth. These issues are of huge importance for social work as a profession that seeks to promote social justice. Social work has not been exempted from cuts in local authority spending, the overall result being that welfare provision has been reduced at a time when it is most required.

The greatest impact of the economic, social and penal policies discussed in this book has, of course, been on the poor. The retrenchment of the welfare state has the greatest impact on those who are in most need of, or most reliant on, it. Austerity has been presented as a response to a national emergency – somehow forced on the coalition. This is disingenuous to say the least. The financial crisis of 2008, or, more accurately, the 2010 general election, provided a political opportunity that was taken by the Tory Party. The Liberal Democrats then provided a fig leaf to the Tories in the coalition, ironically paying the electoral price for the unpopularity of austerity at the 2015 general election.

The wider political climate is thus one that is at best indifferent to social work's expressed professional values, commitment to progressive reform and social justice. I use these terms with their generally accepted meaning rather than the neoliberal or Third Way sense where reform has come to mean cuts. In some senses, this is nothing new. Social work values have never been particularly mainstream ones. It would be odd, particularly in a country as conservative as England, if they were. However, the influence of these wider values is not to be underestimated. For example, on social issues such as gender, race and sexuality, I think that the profession can be rightly proud of the role that it has played in tackling and challenging prejudice and discrimination. What was seen as 'political correctness gone mad' in the late 1980s is now part of the mainstream. I should sound a note of caution here, however, as the Brexit referendum and 2010 and 2015 general elections showed that parties are willing to campaign on an openly racist/anti-immigrant platform. Gordon Brown's 'British jobs for British workers' slogan and Labour selling 'Controls on immigration' mugs are examples of this. There has been a 41 per cent increase in hate crimes since the referendum vote. The idea that we live in a post-racial, post-identity paradise of liberal tolerance is naive in the extreme. Progress has been made, but there is always more work to be done. In addition, recent political events demonstrate that the basis of these gains should never be taken for granted.

The impact on the world of social work can be seen in a number of areas. The increase in inequality has led to greater social, personal and emotional distress. Social workers face increasing workloads at a time when resources are being reduced. Alongside these developments, it should be noted that many social workers have been made redundant or are being asked to do much more with much fewer resources. The day-to-day work of the social work practitioner has inevitably become much more demanding and pressurised. In addition, the nature or focus of social work practice has undergone a change. In adult services and mental health, care management approaches are, to my mind, the complete antithesis of relational social work. They have helped to create a heavily bureaucratic system of risk assessment and care planning. One of the greatest ironies of these developments is that its loudest supporters have presented these moves in the name of choice, independence and 'personalisation' – another fine example of the language of progressive reform being colonised. A similar pattern has occurred in children and families' social work practice where the problems of poverty and inequality have become individualised. The response of the state is to produce a child welfare system that is increasingly authoritarian (Parton, 2014).

Conclusion

One of the key premises of this book is that social work is a political activity – not in the sense of party political, but rather, it is concerned with fundamental issues such as the nature of the relationship between the individual and the state, when the state should intervene in the lives of its citizens, and what constitutes a justice society. Social work is involved in the playing out of these issues not just in national and international forums, but perhaps more importantly in the day-to-day interactions between practitioners and service users. The complex nature of these issues and practitioners' ability to play a part in resolving them or challenging injustice remains one of the key attractions of the profession. Almost without exception, the prospective students that I meet at interview or on open days are committed to social justice in its broadest sense. Social work is a complex, messy business, but it has to be understood within a broader social, political and economic context.

The modern neoliberal state, far from being 'rolled back', has been effectively reconstructed and re-engineered. This book seeks to outline the processes and also the impacts of this re-engineering process, exploring social work's place within this new welfare landscape. The influence of Wacquant and his notion of the 'centaur state' are key to the analysis here. In this model, the state has retreated from some of its traditional roles – most notably the regulation of the market. However, the state is more heavily involved in the lives of some citizens, particularly the urban poor, than previously. The expansion of the use of imprisonment is one area where this is most apparent. Alongside these developments, the left hand of the state has, to use Wacquant's phrase, been colonised by the doxa, tropes techniques and the rationale of the Right. In the concluding chapter, I argue that there is scope for social work to challenge these and to return to a more relation-based approach.

Stuart Hall, who died in February 2014, has proved to be one of the most perceptive and original analysts of neoliberalism. Hall was a cultural and political theorist who examined the impact of the end of the Empire. In a recent memoir, *Familiar stranger*, that traces his journey from Jamaica via Merton College Oxford as a Rhodes scholar to a glittering academic career, he describes himself as 'the last colonial' (Hall, 2017a, p 1). Hall argues that 'hybridity', as he terms it, is one of the key features and impacts of globalisation. He is concerned with how these issues play out in cultural and political settings. In the UK context, he argues that on a very personal level the answer to the question 'Where are you from?' increasingly involves a complex tale of migration from Africa, the Caribbean and Europe. Hall's academic work in the areas of cultural theory, race and racism, the construction of national identities and the importance of the media in framing debates around topics such as crime has been profoundly influential on successive generation of thinkers. His major works, such as *Policing the crisis*, *Culture, media, language* and *The politics of Thatcherism* remain key texts for anyone who seeks to understand modern society and politics. In an interview with *The Guardian* in 2012, Hall outlined the importance of moving away from a political analysis that is solely concerned with the problems of the economy:

> I got involved in cultural studies because I didn't think life was purely economically determined. I took all this up as an argument with economic determinism. I lived my life as an argument with Marxism, and with neoliberalism. Their point is that, in the last instance, economy will determine it. But when is the last instance? If you're analysing the present conjuncture, you can't start and end at the economy. It is necessary, but insufficient.

Hall therefore emphasised that an economic explanation was never simply enough. The importance of cultural and social attitudes could not be overlooked. This is particularly important when exploring the role of social work and its position in welfare provision and its relationship with the state. One of the problems that the profession has consistently faced is a failure to explain to the wider public its role in providing support to vulnerable people and families. This has left it open to a series of lazy stereotypes such as the radical PC social worker detached from the reality of the day-to-day lives of service users. It may come as a shock to readers to know that, in my 30 years as a probation officer, social worker and academic, I have worked with colleagues who hold a broad range of political, social and religious views. The one thing that they had in common was a commitment to working with vulnerable people to tackle the difficulties they face. Unfortunately, the profession still struggles to get this basic message across.

To a certain extent, social work will always remain at odds with the prevailing politics of the day. Surely part of the role of the profession is to advocate for socially marginalised groups? That will inevitably lead to some conflict with the government and policies of the day. I would argue that social work would be failing in one of the key roles of the profession if it did not act in this way. Social work has become increasingly concerned with rational, technocratic and bureaucratic responses. This has clearly been driven in large part by policy and political changes that the social work profession alone cannot possibly prevent. While acknowledging this, social work practitioners and educators have also been somewhat complicit in these moves. For example, the focus on a competency-based approach to the assessment of students led to a bureaucratic rather than a values-based focus. The Professional Capabilities Framework (PCF) offers the opportunity to reverse this trend – this is discussed in more detail in the concluding chapter. I should emphasise that social work is not monolithic. There are many who have been unhappy with these trends and used the creative space that they have carved out to find ways to challenge them. The broad direction of travel has been clear. Social work values have probably been increasingly at odds with those underpinning policy. In addition, as noted above, NPM and other organisational developments have created a practice environment that is overly bureaucratic (Munro, 2011).

In January 1979, Hall published 'The great moving right show' (Hall, 2017b). In this article, he coined the term 'Thatcherism' before, it should be noted, Mrs Thatcher had been elected Prime Minister. Hall was heavily influenced by the work of Gramsci. In this piece he sought to examine the roots of the Right-ward shift that had taken place in British politics. He was one of the first commentators to argue that this 'swing to the Right' could not be ignored, but had to be challenged. Hall suggests that from the late 1960s onwards the state – whatever party was in power – was on a collision course with the labour movement and the working class because of the retrenchment that followed a period of expansion in public services. The Tories fought the 1970 election on a campaign based around social anxieties and the need to restore authority and stand firm against what Enoch Powell had called 'the invisible enemy within' – this predictable list included trade unionists, immigrants, hippies and social workers.

In this essay, Hall unpicks the appeal of Thatcher as a political figure – both she and Reagan were immensely skilled in transforming or reducing the complexities of monetarism to appeal slogans.. Reagan was able to portray 'big government' as the problem, not the solution.

As Hall notes, Thatcher's anti-statism meant that she was able to pose as being 'with the people'. The appeal of anti-collectivism lies in the fact that for many, the state 'is increasingly encountered and experienced by ordinary working people as, indeed, not a beneficiary but a powerful bureaucratic imposition' (Hall, 2017a, p 174). Despite the best efforts of social workers across the country, it must be acknowledged that this is a view that has a great deal of contemporary resonance. It is, of course, somewhat ironic that the greatest increase in the demands of bureaucracy has come under administrations allegedly committed to a smarter, leaner and, many would add, meaner state. Hall concluded that Thatcherism could be seen as a Tory variant of neoliberalism. The Tory elements were clear in the Imperial nostalgia and the production of the persona of the Iron Lady. Gilroy (2002) noted that when Thatcher was at her lowest point in 1982, what rescued her was not market rationality, but a dose of British nationalism in the shape of the Falklands War and its aftermath.

In 1998, Hall wrote what can be seen as a companion essay, 'The great moving nowhere show' (Hall, 2017c). This was written when Blair and New Labour were at the height of their popularity having recently won a landslide general election victory. This is, again, a very perceptive piece. Hall notes that Blair is evidence of the success of the Thatcherite project, in that:

> Its aim was to transform the political landscape, irrevocably: to make us think in and speak its language as if there were no other. (p 283)

In this essay, Hall notes that there are two main traditions that Blair's Third Way seeks to combine. A Left of Centre approach focuses on social solidarity and social provision to provide a buffer against market inequality and instability. Neoliberalism, in contrast, emphasises low taxes, assumes a competitive view of human nature and sees the market as the most effective means of the distribution of resources. On the surface, the Third Way is attractive because, as Hall puts it, it offers a 'politics without enemies'. He also notes that New Labour began a process whereby a language of progressive social justice has been colonised by the Right. Neoliberalism has been very successful in colonising the language of its critics and using this as a basis for renewal (Boltanski and Chiapello, 2005; Fraser, 2009). Thus welfare reform is a term used for the removal of benefits, and this insidious process reached a high point under Iain Duncan Smith's period as Secretary of State for Work and Pensions. New Labour can best be understood as a hybrid, a social democratic variant of neoliberalism. The neoliberal elements are readily apparent with a commitment to lightly regulated markets. In addition, New Labour retreated from the party's historic commitment to universality of social provision. The social democratic aspects are most apparent in the investment in public services, but these are to be delivered via a 'market state'. This led to outsourcing and other features of the audit culture and NPM that will be depressingly familiar to any social worker or colleagues across public services.

The introduction of austerity policies can be seen, in some senses, as the ultimate application of neoliberalism to welfare provision. The narrative that the crisis was the result of an over-generous welfare state created by a profligate New Labour administration was never adequately challenged. This, then, became the starting point for a period of retrenchment in public services that has not been experienced in this country since the Second World War. In fact, as Ken Loach shows in the 'Spirit of 45', the modern welfare state was created when the country faced much more perilous economic circumstances. Between 2008 and 2010, the Brown administration, at the same time as bailing out the banks, maintained a commitment to public spending. In agreeing to enter a coalition government, David Cameron and Nick Clegg argued that the country was facing a national emergency. Hall (2017b, p 175) highlighted that the language and rhetoric of the 'national interest' had been the 'principal ideological form, in which, a succession of defeats have been imposed on the working class.' Those who have had to bear the brunt of the pain that austerity has inflicted are the poorest and most marginalised members of our society. The notion that 'we are all in this together' could just as easily have been coined by another famous George – Orwell, not Osborne.

Social work in the era of neoliberalism and austerity

Neoliberalism as an ideology is now deeply embedded. This is part of its success in that it is so rooted in public discourse that it is both present and absent – present in the sense that, as we have seen, all UK governments have accepted the main premises of market discourse. This is part of the success of the ideological project. However, few, if any, of its main proponents would describe themselves as neoliberal. This is partly due to the famous British distrust of openly expressed ideological positions, but also because loaded terms such as free markets, welfare reform and modernising public services do this ideological work much more effectively.

The broader question that is explored throughout this book is what has been the impact of the neoliberal revolution, or Hall's 'great moving right show', on social work and social work practice? The increased marketisation and managerialism that has been imposed on other areas of the public sector has also cast a blight on social work. Social work and the role of social workers has always been contested. It is in a liminal position. It has elements of both care and control (Hyslop, 2016). Individual workers balance these contradictions in their daily working lives. Webb and Gray (2013) note that neoliberalism has shifted the balance. These changes limit the scope for social workers to establish genuine positive relationships with service users. Hyslop (2016), in his study of social workers in New Zealand, notes the tension between Philp's (1979) notion that social work knowledge and discourse was generated in that indeterminate space between the individual and society and the current informational, procedural risk management approach (Parton, 2014).

There is a gap between social work values and their commitment to the relational and current organisational structures and the dominant discourse of risk. In addition, social workers are working with people or groups – the poor, marginalised, asylum-seekers and refugees – who have been subjected to an almost unremitting process of 'Othering' and demonisation. Ideologies are not all-powerful Leviathans. While recognising that social work faces many challenges in the stormy present, we should also acknowledge that its core values nonetheless remain attractive.

TWO

Class, poverty and inequality

The previous chapter examined the development and expansion of neoliberal ideas. It then went on to look at the recent application of that group of policies – particularly changes to the welfare system and the reduction in the provision of public services – that have come to be known as 'austerity'. This chapter explores the implications for social work practice of the various discourses that explain poverty.

Class

One of the main arguments put forward here is that any consideration or analysis of the causes of poverty are curiously both present and absent in debates about the nature of current social work practice. The emphasis in social work theory is still heavily tilted to psychodynamic explanations at the expense of sociological approaches. Social workers, as Howe (2014) rightly notes, come from a range of theoretical perspectives; this has and always will be the case. (The social, psychological and stigmatising impacts of poverty are examined in more depth in the following chapter.) As I argue throughout this book, there is a need for a refocusing of social work practice. This requires a shift from procedural and risk-driven approaches that have developed as a result of the broader sociological and cultural shifts, allowing for a form of practice that allows social work to meet the ambitious aims of the International Federation of Social Workers' (IFSW) definition of social work as:

> ... a practice-based profession and an academic discipline that promotes social change and development, social cohesion, and the empowerment and liberation of people. Principles of social justice, human rights, collective responsibility and respect for diversities are central to social work. Underpinned by theories of social work, social sciences, humanities and indigenous knowledge, social work engages people and structures to address life challenges and enhance wellbeing. (IFSW, 2000)

There has been an increasing interest in class and related issues, particularly following the economic crisis of 2008. For example, Piketty's *Capital in the 21st century* (2014) has sold over 1.5 million copies. Nine million people completed the Great British Class Survey (Savage et al, 2013). Class is not simply an economic issue. It often seems a particularly British or possibly English obsession. This can be seen in the extent to which political figures such as former Prime Minister David Cameron – a descendent of William IV, educated at Eton, Philosophy, Politics and Economics student at the University of Oxford, and married to the daughter of Viscountess Astor – go to incredible lengths to present themselves as 'ordinary' or 'middle class'. This can lead to embarrassment, for example, when Cameron tried to pass himself off as a lifelong Aston Villa fan. Warner (2015) shows that these claims can have a much greater political impact. In the aftermath of the death of 'Baby P', both Cameron and Ed Balls wrote emotive columns about the case. The starting point was that they were outraged as fathers at the appalling nature of the treatment inflicted on 'Baby P'. In making this claim, they also criticised social workers for being bureaucrats and lacking the common sense to see the real nature of the situation. In so doing, Cameron and Balls were making claims based on their self-proclaimed status as 'ordinary' members of the public. Whereas they were members of a political elite. In these circumstances, they were able to step outside their position to side with the public against 'out of touch' social workers.

The issue of class was an underlying theme of the European referendum debates where the leaders of the Brexit campaign presented themselves as leading a campaign to 'Get our country back' from a liberal elite. This was a very British-style revolution, as the most prominent Brexit campaigners – Nigel Farage (leader of UKIP) and the Conservative Cabinet members Boris Johnson and Michael Gove – had all been privately educated. Farage was a stockbroker and Johnson and Gove journalists for leading Tory-supporting newspapers before entering party politics.

Social work as a profession is committed to social justice, but in the debates exploring social work's theoretical focus on broader identity politics in the 1980s and 1990s, the issue of class was obscured or marginalised. It is important to make clear that my argument should not be seen as supporting those who argue that we are in a post-racial, post-feminist, post-queer society. This is at best naive at worst a reactionary view that seems to argue that all these issues have been 'solved', and that minorities are no longer marginalised but somehow actually enjoy privileged status. My position is that to have any real meaning, social justice requires that all citizens enjoy social, economic and political rights. These themes are explored in the final chapter, which argues that the notion of dignity must be fundamental to recasting the approach to social work.

Poverty and inequality

There is a fundamental divide between those who see poverty as the result of structural failings in modern capitalism and those who see poverty as the result of the individual failings of the poor. As Todd (2010, p 2) notes, the myth that the 'poor caused their own poverty was a persistent one, precisely because it served powerful people's interests.' Todd was writing about the experiences of the working class in the 1930s Britain of mass unemployment and the means test. Since 1979, social policy in the UK has clearly shifted – Todd's myth has become revitalised and reinvigorated, and seems as strong as ever. There was a brief respite during the first years of the Blair government when investment in health, education and other services such as Sure Start was based on a structural analysis. This was, however, combined with a distinctly moralising tone that subsequently began to dominate. The importance of these debates for social work is that the majority of practice takes place in poor areas or with marginalised individuals. Savage (2015) outlines the way that the UK and, by implication, other liberal economies are increasingly socially as well as economically segregated. Wilkinson and Pickett (2009) demonstrate that this inequality has social and psychological as well as economic effects. Put simply, there are huge differences between the physical and mental health of the richest and poorest in society. These differences are starkest in the most unequal societies, and more equal societies, with progressive welfare and health systems, mitigate these potentially adverse outcomes (Marmot, 2010).

Piketty (2015) of the modern development of capitalism outlines that the current levels of inequality have not been seen for over a hundred years. He argues that there has been a revival of what he terms a 'patrimonial class', an economic elite that has mostly obtained its wealth via inheritance rather than through innovation in the development of new goods and services. This class has been called the 1 per cent – although there are actually huge disparities in wealth even in this group. Milanovic (2016) outlines the rise of what he terms a 'global plutocracy'. This group of super-wealthy individuals is, in some senses, divorced from the national politics of the group in which they happen to be resident. They clearly influence policy, but seem immune to any government attempts to control them.

Poverty

The modern study of poverty begins with the work of Booth in 1880s London. The arguments that this work generated and the themes within it remain with us today. The rapid industrial development of the 1850s, including the expansion of the railways and the establishment of the modern factory system, saw the creation of great wealth alongside concentrations of urban poverty. At this point, poverty was widely viewed as the result of individual failings. As Stedman-Jones (2013) notes in the later Victorian period, the poor were feared mainly because they were seen as a real physical threat to the middle classes.

Charles Booth was born in Liverpool, and his family were wealthy shipping and corn merchants. Booth campaigned as a Liberal candidate in the 1865 election, appalled by the extent and nature of the urban poverty that he encountered. He subsequently moved to London, and in the 1880s carried out his famous study of poverty, producing detailed maps of the streets of London. (These documents can be viewed at http://booth.lse.ac.uk) On these maps, Booth produced an analysis of the class structure of the time, marking areas as follows:

> Black: Lowest class. Vicious, semi-criminal.
> Dark Blue: Very poor, casual. Chronic want.
> Light Blue: Poor. 18s. to 21s. a week for a moderate family.
> Purple: Mixed. Some comfortable others poor.
> Pink: Fairly comfortable. Good ordinary earnings.
> Red: Middle class. Well-to-do.
> Yellow: Upper-middle and Upper classes. Wealthy.

In the first volume of the poverty series in the final edition of *Life and labour of the people in London*, Booth (1903) developed an eight-stage system for categorisation. This is worth outlining in some depth here as it combines economic themes.

Table 2.1: Booth's class profiles

Category	Description
A	The lowest class that consists of some occasional labourers, street sellers, loafers, criminals and semi-criminals. Their life is the life of savages, with vicissitudes of extreme hardship and their only luxury is drink
B	Casual earnings, very poor. The labourers do not get as much as three days' work a week, but it is doubtful if many could or would work full time for long together if they had the opportunity. Class B is not one in which men are born and live and die so much as a deposit of those who, from mental, moral and physical reasons, are incapable of better work.
C	Intermittent earnings; 18s to 21s per week for a moderate family. The victims of competition and on them falls with particular severity the weight of recurrent depressions of trade. Labourers, poorer artisans and street sellers. This irregularity of employment may show itself in the week or in the year: stevedores and waterside porters may secure only one or two days' work in a week, whereas labourers in the building trades may get only eight or nine months in a year.
D	Small regular earnings; poor, regular earnings. Factory, dock, and warehouse labourers, carmen, messengers and porters. Of the whole section none can be said to rise above poverty, nor are many to be classed as very poor. As a general rule they have a hard struggle to make ends meet, but they are, as a body, decent steady men, paying their way and bringing up their children respectably.
E	Regular standard earnings, 22s to 30s per week for regular work, fairly comfortable. As a rule the wives do not work, but the children do: the boys commonly following the father, the girls taking local trades or going out to service.
F	Higher-class labour and the best paid of the artisans. Earnings exceed 30s per week. Foremen are included, city warehousemen of the better class and first hand lightermen; they are usually paid for responsibility and are men of good character and much intelligence.
G	Lower middle class. Shopkeepers and small employers, clerks and subordinate professional men. A hardworking sober, energetic class.
H	Upper middle class, servant keeping class.

As Savage (2016) notes, the Booth model has remained influential, and in some senses, it casts a shadow over subsequent studies of poverty. In the 1940s, work in the US sought to remove the moral dimension from the approach that Booth pioneered. Studies such as that by the Lynds (1929, 1937) took a wider view of the factors that influence social stratification. Edwards (1943) developed a classification scheme for the US Census that was based on socioeconomic status, and his scheme had the following categories:

- Professional, technical, and kindred workers
- Managers and administrators
- Sales workers
- Clerical workers
- Craftsmen
- Operatives
- Labourers, except farmers
- Farmworkers

Socioeconomic status combines not just income but also education and occupational prestige. This recognises that social status is not simply a matter of economic position and vice versa.

These measures of social stratification are closely linked to employment. They lack subtlety in that there is a lack of sophistication in examining the actual status within professions. This is increasingly relevant. There are actually very significant differences between employees or professionals who nominally have the same title – for example a commercial lawyer working in the city is not in the same class or social position as a lawyer working in a law centre. Another key weakness is that other factors are ignored that are pivotal in the creation of social status and also identity – race and gender being two that are not taken into account here. This focus on employment status as the defining factor in socioeconomic status means that this model struggles to take account of the roles of groups that are not part of the regulated economy or in formal paid employment. The criticisms of postcolonial and feminist thought is that this approach masks the underlying racist and patriarchal nature of modern capitalism. The lives of black and female workers and their key role in the functioning of modern economies is minimised, or not even considered (Gilroy, 2002; Emejulu, 2008; Fraser, 2013b).

In the 1960s, the British sociologist John Goldthorpe (2010) sought to explore the impact of social mobility and whether the traditional notion of class had outlived its usefulness as an analytical tool. His study of the 'affluent worker' examined the impact of the post-war economic boom and the beginning of the shifts in the economy that saw new patterns of employment. Goldthorpe argued that the traditional working, middle and upper class model of stratification had been overtaken because these divides were less clear. Workers were now enjoying access to goods and services such as cars, televisions and foreign holidays that had once been seen as indicators of a secure middle-class position. Goldthorpe developed a model with 11 social groups that was eventually adopted by the Office for National

Statistics (ONS). This approach looks at the new reality of the post-war consumer society. However, it was much weaker at examining the social, cultural and political impacts of these huge changes, one of the most significant being the fact that the traditional political base of parties of the Left – the trade union movement – lost its power. More fluid patterns of working make it more difficult for new workers to be recruited to unions. The social changes almost meant that class allegiances were more fluid. It might have become cool to be working class or invent working-class roots in the Arts from the 1960s onwards, but in other areas, the consumer society was very much driven by middle-class modes of consumption (Todd, 2010).

The political implications of these debates about the nature and significance of class are vitally important. However, they also have psychological and individual implications, as they are a key factor in the creation of a social identity, although it should be recognised that they are only one part of that identity and are not static. I mean this in two senses. First, they change overtime, but also individuals challenge traditional notions, and by doing so help to shape new class identities. One of the paradoxes of neoliberal individualism is that it attempts to deny the existence of class – we are all individuals – while at the same time the impact of its social policies serves to reinforce class divisions. Class has become more significant at a time when political parties seek to avoid any debates that are premised on its existence. Those on the Left who raise issues in these terms are always accused of the politics of envy. The result is that progressive parties have developed a whole new language of social exclusion to avoid discussing class, poverty and inequality as issues of social justice. These issues are now debated in technocratic terms or with a focus on a very small group of concerns. For example, debates in education are overwhelmingly examined through a lens of how many state-educated children go on to study at Oxbridge or very occasionally the whole of the Russell Group of Universities. This debate covers the huge disparities in state education and also ignores the experiences of other groups.

Bourdieu's analysis of class

Bourdieu's (2010) analysis of class has become the most influential in modern sociological approaches. His work is complex and challenging, foregrounding notions of class and social stratification, so it can be viewed as both a challenge and response to the dominant post-modernist discourse of identity or risk that seems to view class, in Beck's (1992, 2008) terms, as a 'zombie category'. Bourdieu's work, as well as reinvigorating debates about the value of class as an analytical tool, provides a framework for exploring its continuing influence. A staunch opponent of neoliberalism and what he saw as its destruction of the social state, Bourdieu was concerned with the ways in which elites reproduced and also reinforced their own positions. This was of particular interest, as public discourses seemed committed to a more egalitarian culture and society. Bourdieu is clearly one of the most influential and important sociologists of the past 50 years. His key concepts and ideas have opened up new approaches to the analysis of education and television, and also our notions of class and identity. Discussions of Bourdieu, while acknowledging his undoubted intellectual brilliance, influence and glittering academic career, often refer to his humble origins as 'the son of a postal worker and his wife'. This rather underlines one of his key arguments about the importance, but also the denial, of the influence of class in modern societies. Rarely, if ever, does a similar discussion of Michel Foucault, a man of equally dazzling intellect and influence, refer to the fact that he was 'the son of a surgeon'.

Bourdieu's analysis examines the ongoing influence of class in modern liberal democracies. One feature of these societies is that in the wider social discourse there is a commitment to social equality, but this does not reflect the reality of those societies. As the discussion of class decreased, class structures have become more deeply entrenched. Bourdieu was a noted critic of neoliberalism, particularly its attack on the structure and delivery of public services. His analysis of class weaves together the influence of economic and other social factors.

Savage (2016) outlines Bourdieu's *Capital, assets and resources*. Bourdieu's model of capitals identifies three types – economic, cultural and social. Economic capital is largely self-explanatory – financial assets, income and investments and so on. Bourdieu then went on to examine the impact of what he termed cultural and social capital. He examined the influence of social networks among elites and also the ways in which these networks, alongside cultural activities, could be used to create advantage. In these processes, education has a clear role to play. Parents who have the greatest economic and cultural capital are able to use these resources to ensure that their children gain access to the most prestigious establishments. Elite schools and universities not only reinforce existing social divisions; they enable elites to create the social connections that will serve them well in adult and professional life. Bourdieu terms these working-class children like himself, who make it against the odds to elite schools and universities, *les miracules*. He also highlights the ways in which working-class children may feel

42

stigmatised when they enter these essentially middle-class spaces, often lacking or feeling they lack the cultural language or references – music, newspapers, television programmes, for example. The move into this sort of environment can be a dislocating and confidence-destroying one for young working-class children. Hanley (2012, 2016) discusses such experiences. She outlines the ways that as a working class pupil she felt isolated at every stage of her academic career. This continued in her journalist career. She shows the way that she feels that she was made to feel embarrassed about her background. In her work, she describes herself as feeling like an imposter on occasions.

Bourdieu's work, by linking the economic with broader social attitudes, seeks to provide an analysis of patterns of cultural consumption. Goldthorpe's analysis did not address these issues (such as newspaper readership or other interests). Bourdieu outlines the ways in which the social world is a system of power relations and also a symbolic system. Taste or cultural preferences are not simply neutral; they become a basis for social judgement. An appreciation of so-called high culture – art, opera and classical music – becomes the marker of the membership of an elite. In addition, attendance at galleries, classical music concerts and so on provide opportunities to mix with fellow members of an elite. Milanovic (2016) has been critical of Bourdieu for his emphasis on the importance of elite cultural activities, which is seen as a particularly French approach. Milanovic argues that post-modernism has seen the collapse of the high and popular culture divide – the awarding of the Nobel Prize for Literature to Bob Dylan could be used to support this. Milanovic suggests that these cultural shifts have seen the emergence of what he calls the 'cultural omnivore' – someone who appreciates and is interested in both elite and popular culture, who is interested in modern novels, 'Strictly Come Dancing', the latest Blockbuster film and sport. The gentrification of sport – football in particular – is a particular manifestation of these trends. For example, recent Prime Ministers Major, Blair, Brown and Cameron, in an attempt to establish their 'regular guy' credentials, all tried fairly unconvincingly to claim that they had a lifelong interest in the game. The emergence of celebrity culture has been a key feature in these processes. Cultural omnivores do exist, but whether they are to be found outside of the intellectual and media elites is a matter of some debate.

Poverty and inequality: Recent trends and approaches

Defining poverty

Backwith (2015) notes that the definition of poverty is problematic, but also that any definition adopted carries within it an approach to the resolution of the problems that it creates. There will always be those who argue that modern society has abolished poverty – the argument being encapsulated in the idea that if someone has a television, then they cannot possibly be considered poor. The initial modern surveys – Booth's in London and Rowntree's in York – were based on absolute or subsistence definitions of poverty. The poor were those who did not have sufficient money to meet their material needs. Rowntree (2014) argued that 'primary poverty' should be defined in such a way that individuals did not have sufficient resources to meet their basic needs – food, shelter and clothing – for the maintenance of physical health. Backwith (2015) argues that Rowntree's definition was deliberately harsh so as to raise awareness of the issues of poverty. It also had the perhaps unintended consequence of seeing poverty solely in terms of income rather than in broader notions of citizenship. This approach has bedevilled debates about poverty ever since. The focus on purely physical resources ignores or excludes many of the elements of what would now be viewed as essential to wellbeing or being able to play an active role in society.

Poverty, at the subsistence level, clearly exists across the modern world. The success of the post-war welfare state was largely seen to have eradicated poverty of this nature from the UK. However, Townsend's work meant that poverty was rediscovered in the 1960s. Townsend redefined poverty in relative terms. In this schema, poverty meant that individuals or families lacked the resources to follow the customary diet, take part in a broad range of social activities or live in the conditions that the majority of that society live in. This approach acknowledges that poverty is not static and will change over time. Townsend's work involved trying to identify what were the necessities of modern life in the creation of a poverty index. This method implicitly acknowledges that items that might once have been seen as luxuries – a car, computer or mobile phone – almost inevitably become essentials in modern life. The increasing complexity of the modern world requires that definitions of poverty allow for these changes, or we are trapped in a subsistence view of poverty. This is very limiting, but also marginalises the reality of modern poverty as well as the experiences of individuals.

Social exclusion

In 1992, the late John Smith became leader of the Labour Party. Labour had narrowly, but surprisingly, lost the 1992 election, so faced another period in opposition. Smith began the process of developing new, potentially election-winning, policies by establishing a Commission for Social Justice headed by Sir Gordon Borrie (1994). Reflecting Smith's own roots in the Scottish Labour Party, the commission was committed to a vision of social equality, outlining its key principles of its vision of social justice as follows:

- equal worth of all citizens
- equal right to be able to meet their basic needs
- need to spread opportunities and life chances as widely as possible
- the requirement that we reduce and where possible eliminate unjustified inequalities

It is the reflection of the Right-wards shift in UK politics that these essentially centrist, socially democratic principles, in the current context, appear radical. Smith died of a heart attack in 1994 and was succeeded by Tony Blair. Blair's creation of New Labour was then an attempt to create a new political approach that married a dynamic laissez-faire economy with greater investment in public services. In 1997, New Labour faced an environment where there had been significant under-investment in public services – in particular, the NHS – for some time, with a third of the UK population living in poverty. The new government sought to move towards a new attitude and approach to poverty and inequality, and coined the term 'social exclusion'. This was a classic New Labour combination of structural and individual factors, including unemployment, low income, poor housing, high crime environments, family breakdown and poor skills. Social exclusion as a term was positive in that it captured the overall impact of the increase in inequality that had occurred over the previous 18 years of Tory government. However, it is also a term that de-politicised notions of inequality. The Blairite mantra was that equality of opportunity rather than equality of outcome should be the concern of progressive governments. This period saw greater investment in public services and social programmes such as Sure Start that were aimed at tackling childhood inequalities.

Modern poverty

Recent detailed work from the Joseph Rowntree Foundation (JRF, 2016) has analysed the nature of modern poverty. It starts from the position that poverty is dynamic, that individuals and families may experience short periods of poverty. Those living in or at the edge of poverty often lack the resources to deal with unexpected life events. An accident at work, a large utility bill or being the victim of a burglary can have disproportionate effects on those who do not have access to networks or support to tackle the aftermaths of such events. JRF outlines that poverty has changed significantly over the past 10 years, and the biggest shift has been towards a rise in poverty among young people. Conversely, positive changes in the pensions system mean that there has been a significant fall in poverty among older people, that is, those over 75. As JRF notes, the majority of those now living in poverty are in working families, concluding that 13.5 million people are living in poverty; 7.9 million are working-age adults, 3.9 million are children and 1.6 million are pensioners; 39 per cent of those living in poverty are members of a family where one person is disabled; and 35 per cent of children in poverty live in a lone-parent family. Relative income poverty is set at 60 per cent of median household income, adjusted for family size.

Inequality

The banking crisis and the response of governments to the crisis seems to have generated a new wave of interest in the impact of poverty and inequality. A book at the forefront of this research is *The spirit level: Why equality is better for everyone*, by Wilkinson and Pickett (2009). One of the weaknesses of the relative approach to the measurement of poverty is that its opponents can argue that on the terms put forward by its proponents, poverty will always exist. Whatever measure is chosen, there will always be some citizens who have this level of income. One solution to this is to consider inequality rather than measures of poverty. This approach has become more popular and will be examined in more depth in the next chapter. Writers such as Dorling (2015) and Sayer (2015) examine the ways in which modern capitalism operates to create and sustain deeply divisive and socially unjust levels of inequality. These works show that the claims of trickle-down neoliberal economics that unrestrained market capitalism would lead to higher standards of living for all ring increasingly hollow. Hall commented (in *The Guardian*; see Adams, 2013) that both neoliberalism and Marxism share a belief that ultimately economics is sovereign. For Hall, this ignores the importance of cultural and social attitudes. Friedman (2002) claimed that markets are not interested in colour, creed or race, because exchange is a purely monetary function. This ignores the social context in which the market operates. For example, Friedman, writing in a racially divided society, seemed able to overlook that some businesses would refuse to serve or sell goods and services to African Americans. Wilkinson and Pickett (2009) argue that just reducing inequality is not just a matter of social justice; it is in the interests of all citizens, even wealthier ones, as more equal societies are healthier. Better health and social outcomes are produced for all citizens across a wide range of measures. These ideas are based on notions of social reciprocity, mutual obligation and community ties that are deeply attractive to those who share a commitment to social work's expressed value base.

Wilkinson and Pickett outline three potential measures of inequality:

- Income inequality: the extent to which income is distributed unevenly in a group of people.
- Pay inequality: income is distributed unevenly in a group of people.
- Wealth inequality: wealth refers to the total amount of assets of an individual or household. This may include financial assets, such as bonds and stocks, property and private pension rights.

The spirit level is concerned with the relative positions of all citizens within any given society. The Gini coefficient measures inequality across the whole of society rather than simply comparing different income groups. Corrado Gini, the Italian statistician and sociologist, developed the measure. If all the income went to a single person (maximum inequality) and everyone else got nothing, the Gini coefficient would be equal to 1. If income was shared equally, and everyone got exactly the same, the Gini coefficient would equal 0. Therefore, the lower the Gini coefficient value, the more equal a society.

Most OECD countries have a coefficient lower than 0.32, with the lowest being 0.24, as shown in Figure 2.1. The UK, a fairly unequal society, scores 0.35, and the US, an even more unequal society, 0.39. Denmark, a much more equal society, scores 0.25. Figure 2.1 shows that the countries with the most comprehensive social and welfare provisions are the most equal. This is the result of the redistributive nature of the taxation systems within these countries. These levels of personal taxation pay for the public services that all sectors of society use. One of the most corrosive effects of neoliberal social policy has been to weaken the notion of social or public provision. In effect, this privatisation of social spaces helps to create and then reinforce social division.

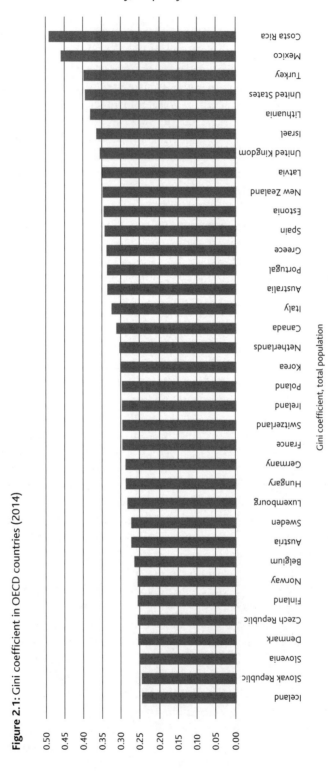

Figure 2.1: Gini coefficient in OECD countries (2014)

Gini coefficient, total population

Source: OECD (2017) Income inequality (indicator). doi: 10.1787/459aa7f1-en (Accessed on 28 September 2017)

The most commonly used definition of poverty in the UK is a relative measure: poverty is defined as having a household income (adjusted for family size) that is less than 60 per cent of median income. This is one of the agreed international measures used throughout the EU. Inequality, by contrast, is always a relative term. It refers to:

> ... the difference between levels of living standards, income etc across the whole economic distribution. In practice, poverty and inequality often rise and fall together but this need not necessarily be the case. Inequality can be high in a society without high levels of poverty due to a large difference between the top and the middle of the income spectrum. (The Equality Trust, nd)

Figure 2.2 shows the Gini coefficient values for just over 50 years, from 1961 to 2015/16. These raw figures have to be treated with some caution. For example, these are measures of economic equality, so take no account of social, legal or civic rights. The UK of the 1960s may well have been a more economically equal country, but it clearly systematically denied full citizenship to a number of its inhabitants – women, minority ethnic groups and gay and lesbian people being among the most obvious examples. In addition, a reduction in the Gini coefficient does not mean that there are not huge individual disparities or that there are groups that face greater risks of poverty. Bearing those caveats in mind, it shows that the UK was much more equal in 1962 that it was in 2012. Ironically, the late 1970s held up by the Right as a period of social and industrial chaos was also the period when the UK was a more equal society.

In *The spirit level*, Wilkinson and Pickett use the following social and health outcomes as measures of the impact of inequality:

- physical health (life expectancy)
- mental health/illness
- drug and alcohol addiction
- imprisonment rates
- obesity
- social mobility
- level of trust
- homicides
- teenage birth rate
- infant mortality

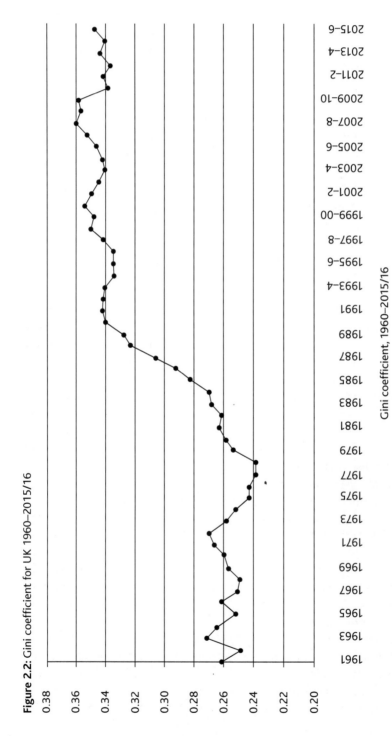

Figure 2.2: Gini coefficient for UK 1960–2015/16

Gini coefficient, 1960–2015/16

Source: The Equality Trust, www.equalitytrust.org.uk/how-has-inequality-changed (Accessed on 28 September 2017)

By measuring across a range of social and health domains, they demonstrate that societies with a policy aimed at increasing equality alongside the public provision of services are healthy, more peaceful and have better educated citizens. This is not to deny that there are social and other difficulties in these countries – to do so would be foolish and naive. The success of the social democratic welfare model has been put under increasing pressure by the forces of globalised capital. In addition, the migrant crisis in Europe in the summer of 2015, despite the initially optimistic response from the German government in particular, highlighted that the Right and neo-Fascist parties are able to effectively combine anti-immigrant and welfare discourses for electoral gain. This process was repeated in the UK Euro referendum by the Brexit campaign.

Health inequalities are one of the most startling outcomes of poverty and social inequality. Put simply, the poorer you are, the more likely you are to experience poor health. There is an interconnectedness here, as long-term health conditions – for example, mental health conditions – are also likely to have an impact on your income and earning power. The World Health Organization (WHO) has defined the social determinants of health as the 'conditions in which people are born, grow, live, work and age. These circumstances are shaped by the distribution of money, power and resources at global, national and local levels' (WHO, 2012).

Health inequalities can be defined as differences in health status or in the distribution of health determinants between different population groups. Differences in mortality rates between people from different social classes would be an example of these processes. This form of inequality does not necessarily constitute inequity. Some health inequalities are attributable to biological variations or free choice. For example, decisions about whether to smoke or levels of alcohol consumption are ones that individual citizens make. However, governments can strongly influence these decisions by a range of public health matters – banning smoking, taxes or fixed unit pricing for alcohol being three popular methods. There are other factors, for example, air pollution, exposure to hazardous working conditions or lack of social amenities that impact on individuals, exposure that is outside of their control.

Sir Michael Marmot's work has been key to understanding differential health outcomes and the link between these and poverty. People living in the poorest neighbourhoods will, on average, die seven years earlier than people living in the richest neighbourhoods (Marmot, 2010). These health inequalities are not just limited to life expectancy but also infant mortality, mental health and physical health – all key measures for Wilkinson and Pickett.

Professor Marmot has helped to produce a tube map to illustrate the impact of health inequalities. *Lives on the line* shows variation in life expectancy in areas across London (Cheshire and O'Brien, 2012).

Professor Marmot was quoted as follows: the map 'captures how stark the health equalities are in a very small geographical area'. He went on to suggest that:

> If you want to see a difference in life expectancy between countries of 11 years, you can fly from London to Guatemala. But if you are worried about your carbon footprint, you could just catch the Tube east. The difference between Hackney and the West End is the same as the difference between England and Guatemala in terms of life expectancy. (Dangerfield, 2012, np)

He then added that life expectancy was affected by 'early child development, education, employment and working conditions, having the minimum income to live a healthy life, the environment and the issues of smoking, obesity, drinking and diet.'

The importance of the social provision of health and welfare services has been most vividly demonstrated during the period of austerity. In April 2012, Greece was shocked by the suicide of a 77-year-old pensioner, a retired pharmacist who shot himself outside the Parliament building in Athens. In a note he stated that he had decided to end his life as he did not want to be reduced to foraging in bins for food. The suicide encapsulated the despair of many of the older generation in Greece. In this period of imposed austerity, pensions and other benefits were cut by up to 25 per cent as part of the conditions of the loans that the government received to tackle the sovereign debt crisis. Greece cut its health service budget by 40 per cent. More than 600 Greek citizens killed themselves in 2012. Before the Great Recession, Greece had the lowest suicide rate in Europe; now that rate has doubled. And Greece is not alone. Suicides in other EU countries had been dropping consistently for over 20 years, until the Great Recession (Stuckler and Basu, 2013).

Social work and poverty

It seems a statement of the obvious that social work should be concerned with the nature and impact of poverty. If social work is a profession that is really committed to notions of social justice, then it needs to address these issues. However, one of the key arguments of this book is that social work in England and Wales has moved away from these fundamental areas. Social work is in a liminal position – it is both an organ of the state, but at the same time, it seeks to be part of a process of social change. Bourdieu's (1998) analysis of the state divided its functions into two – the right hand and the left hand. In this schema, the right hand represents policing, law and order, and so on, while the left hand is associated with welfare functions such as health and education. These positions are not fixed, and social work is a profession that can be seen to move between these poles, both on an individual practice and organisational level. Garrett (2013) argues that Bourdieu's polarity fails to take account of the fact that state agencies often have much more ambiguous roles than is sometimes acknowledged. For example, policing is about much more than the prevention of crime and the apprehension of offenders. As social workers know from their daily practice, police officers are involved in a number or areas that relate to the general welfare of citizens – for example, responding to mental health crises (Cummins and Edmondson, 2015). In the same way, state welfare agencies clearly have a 'policing' or interventionist role in the management of what can be broadly termed 'deviant' behaviour. There is a tension between these two roles, a tension that social work often seems reluctant to acknowledge or debate.

One of the many social work myths is that all practitioners share the same (radical) political perspective. A problem that the profession has consistently faced is a failure to explain to the wider public its role in providing support to vulnerable people and families. This has left it open to a series of lazy stereotypes such as the radical PC social worker detached from the reality of the day-to-day lives of service users. In my 30 years as a probation officer, social worker and academic, I have worked with colleagues who hold a broad range of political, social and religious views. Following Howe's model, social workers' theoretical approach will be a key factor in the approach that they take, and also possibly the areas or organisations in which they choose to work. This will be as true in responses to poverty as it will be for other areas. Mantle and Backwith (2010) identify three very broad approaches and responses to the issues of poverty. A critical or radical social work perspective sees the causes of poverty as lying in capitalism, while a systems approach seeks to link individuals to community resources and networks. The final approach that can be termed a bureaucratic or functionalist one focuses on individuals or families. Bureaucratic approaches have become more dominant in recent times.

The IFSW definition of social work contains an implicit view that poverty is a structural problem rather than the result of individual failings of the poor. These explanations seem at odds with my own and colleagues' recent experiences of discussing these issues with social work students and newly qualified staff. This is impressionistic rather than based on empirical research, but it seems to me that what might be termed 'harsher' attitudes to the poor have become much more common. Social work as a discipline has historically been much more attracted to psychodynamic theoretical approaches than sociological ones. The largely uncritical acceptance, dominance and misuse of Attachment Theory is testament to this. Gilligan's work (2007) indicated that around 50 per cent of applicants to social work programmes held views that explained poverty in individual rather than structural terms. The importance of this is not that views should exclude people from the profession – this would be a ridiculous proposition. However, it does highlight that social work is not, as is often portrayed, a hotbed of politically correct radicalism. More importantly, those that see the causes of poverty in these terms will not be attracted to the radical restructuring of society, and are unlikely to be persuaded that this one of the core roles of the social work profession. Ritter (2006) highlighted that some social workers have very negative views of the poor – not that far removed from the underclass discourse.

These tensions play themselves out in practice and academic discussions and seminars on a daily basis, and this final section attempts to demonstrate that it is possible to resolve some of the issues. It is grounded in the belief that good social work practice has to concern itself with the material living conditions of the community and individuals it serves. In this regard, the role of social work has to be seen as individual, local, national and international. The interconnectedness of the modern world means that war or civil strife create a migrant crisis that requires a social work response – either as part of its internationalist role or because refugee communities need support. Strier and Binyamin (2013) argue that poverty can be defined in terms of the domination of a stigmatised group. Therefore, social work practice, if it is to be truly anti-oppressive, needs to be involved in challenging these processes. The work of the late Bob Holman on the Easterhouse Estate in Glasgow is a shining example of the way that social work can rediscover the role outlined in the curiously radical but also dated language of Seebohm (1968):

> ... a wider conception of social service, directed to the well-being of the whole community and not only of social

casualties and seeing the community it serves as the basis of its authority, resources and effectiveness.

This would lead to a model that sees social workers playing a role in developing community resources and assets – social capital, in Bourdieu's terms – such as credit unions, social clubs and activities for young people, while at the same time campaigning on broader social policy issues such as cuts to welfare benefits for people living with disabilities. Alongside this community development role, social workers could work alongside individuals living in poverty to mitigate these issues. Monnickendam et al (2010) emphasise that these issues are one of the fundamental dilemmas in social work practice. The profession's self-proclaimed grand mission of social change is actually achieved in individuals' lives. Thus change takes place on a micro level. Social work clearly plays a role on a macro level in the way that the profession's leaders influence or attempt to shape government policy. However, these realms are far removed from social workers facing the challenges of working with increasingly limited resources.

Conclusion

Stedman-Jones (2004) notes that debates about the nature of poverty have been a consistent feature of modern capitalism since its inception. These complex debates can be divided into two very broad approaches – individual and structural. The modern version of the individual causes of poverty is underclass theory. This sees poverty as a result of the individual moral failings of the poor. This work is most closely associated with Murray (1990, 1994, 2012). In this analysis, poverty is the result of the anti-social behaviour and poor decision-making of the poor, who are unable to hold down regular work and waste resources. These views appear to be deeply entrenched cultural stereotypes that are exploited and reinforced by the tabloid media. A structural analysis locates the maintenance of inequality and poverty in the nature of modern capitalism. The impact of neoliberalism has been to increase inequality but also to shred the social safety net that the post-war welfare state created.

Poverty is a hugely important issue for social work. Its professional ethical base makes an explicit commitment to social justice. In Resolution 21/11, the United Nations (UN) (United Nations General Assembly, 2012) calls for states to eliminate extreme poverty, although there are huge debates about what is meant by 'extreme poverty'. However, there is an increase in the UK of, for example, homelessness and the use of food banks, surely measures of such poverty in a modern society. Poverty and attempts to overcome it, are fundamentally concerned with issues of human rights and equality. Social work can tackle these issues on both individual and organisational levels.

As a profession, social work allies itself with other progressive organisations to campaign against policies that increase poverty and inequality. The work of Bywaters and others is a fine example of the ways that academic research can be used in these arguments (Bywaters et al, 2016). However, overall, the leadership of the social work profession has been disappointingly quiet about the impact of poverty on individuals and communities. Practitioners can work alongside individuals and communities to develop social capital and challenge the stigma that is attached to those living in poverty.

THREE

Advanced marginality and stigma

This chapter examines the social and psychological impacts on poverty and inequality through the concepts of 'advanced marginality' and 'stigma'. The analysis of social stigma is influenced by Wacquant's argument that the 'underclass' discourse not only corrodes social ties, but also the sense of self-worth of the residents of the poorest areas and communities. The majority of social work takes place in these communities, where high rates of poverty, few social resources and amenities, poor housing, high rates of crime and problems such as substance misuse are common.

Wacquant uses Goffman (1963) and Bourdieu et al (1999) as the starting point for his analysis of the development and impact of stigma. Goffman (1963, p 3) describes stigma as an 'attribute that is deeply discrediting.' He goes on to suggest that this attribute reduces the holder 'from a whole and usual person to a tainted, discounted one.' Wacquant explores the ways that these neighbourhoods have become 'terra non grata'. He argues that what he terms new 'anti-ghettos' carry with them the same negative social connotations of the ghetto. Anti-ghetto is used by Wacquant as a term to describe the poorest areas of urban communities. Neoliberalism creates economic and social insecurity. This makes it difficult, if not impossible, for the social and community institutions to survive.

This chapter begins with an exploration of the term 'underclass', before going on to outline the notion and implications of the term 'advanced marginality'. It moves from these sociological perspectives via an outline of Goffman's notion of stigma (1963) to consider the ways in which images of the poor and marginalised are reproduced and serve to reinforce long-standing prejudices. There is a danger in challenging the underclass discourse that progressives replace it with another stereotype of the passive but heroic poor. Throughout this book there is recognition that class identities, like other labels, are not fixed; they are fluid and complex, constantly negotiated and redefined by individuals and groups.

The development of an 'underclass' discourse

Williams describes his influential work, *Keywords* (2014, p 1), thus:

> It is not a dictionary or glossary of a particular academic
> subject. It is not a series of footnotes to dictionary histories
> or definitions of a number of words. It is, rather, the record
> of an inquiry into a vocabulary.

Williams interrogates the roots of the modern usage of words including
culture, industry and nature. As he notes in his introduction, these are
all terms whose meaning has shifted and continues to do so. At the same
time, these phrases are often used in arguments or public discourse in a
very haphazard or lax fashion. Unfortunately, Williams did not include
'underclass' in *Keywords*, and a modern version of such a political and
cultural lexicon would not be complete without its inclusion. It has
become a key term in debates about modern social problems.

There have been debates about the causes, nature and impact of
poverty since the development of modern capitalist societies. The
development of Social Darwinism in the 1880s and 1890s saw political
concerns with what was termed the 'residuum' (Stedman-Jones, 2014).
There were clearly concerns about the welfare of people who were
living in poverty – particularly children. The late Victorian period saw
the establishment of the modern charity sector and also the first shoots
of what might be termed social work – for example, the Settlement
Movement that established Toynbee Hall, in 1884, to provide housing
and education for poor workers in the East End of London (see www.
toynbeehall.org.uk/toynbee-hall-archives).

The broader political concerns were twofold. The first was that
poorer sections of society were having too many children, resulting
in not only increased demands on society, but also a belief that society
would be contaminated and weakened by the behaviour of the poor.
A belief in eugenics and social hygiene to ensure that society was not
producing too many 'imbeciles' or 'inadequates' was a commonly held
and respectable one. Public figures such as George Bernard Shaw and
Winston Churchill were both in favour of these policies (Carey, 2012).

Although the language of this time now appears to most of us as
offensive, the underlying ideas have not disappeared; they have simply
been cast in modern form, which makes them no less offensive or anti-
humanitarian. For example, Perkins (2016), inspired by Eysenck, put
forward the proposition that the welfare state provides incentives for
the least capable (that is, the poorest) parents to have more children.

He goes on to suggest that these children are much more likely to be neglected, thus placing further burdens on society. In putting forward these arguments, which are presented as new and challenging, he portrayed himself as an outsider tackling political correctness and vested interests. In fact, he was giving a modern pseudo-scientific gloss to an argument that would have been heard around many Victorian dinner tables. Similar arguments were presented by Caspi et al (2016), who argued that it was possible to identify future criminals and those who place the greatest demand on welfare services – note the elision of welfare and criminality – by means of a simple test at the age of three.

Welshman (2013) provides an excellent outline of the shifting nature of the attitudes and policy concerns that have underpinned responses to poverty over the past 150 years. This is not to suggest that the social residuum of the 1880s and the underclass of the 1980s and 1990s can be viewed as the same phenomena or variants of the same. Using Williams' approach, these terms need to be interrogated. The argument here is that each term has to be understood in its social, political and historical context, and that earlier terms play into the development of later ones. Thus social residuum is part of the history of the modern term and usage of 'underclass'.

In Booths study outlined in Chapter 1, the lowest class, Class A, was not necessarily seen as presenting an imminent social danger or threat. In coining the term the 'submerged tenth' to refer to those living in permanent poverty, Booth, founder of the Salvation Army, was clearly trying to highlight the need for society to tackle these issues. Poverty was a structural issue but one that led to concerns about the behaviour of the poor. There was thus a moral duty to tackle these issues. The title of his book, *In darkest England and the way out* (1890), is an early modern example of the way that poorer areas of cities are equated with unexplored hostile lands, and there are clear racial overtones to the title. The metaphor of the city or the poorest areas of the city as 'a jungle' continues to be powerful, and there are several consequences to this. It plays into the notion that the poor are, somehow, a class or even a race apart. It suggests that poor areas are sources of danger. And it casts the researcher, social worker and other welfare professionals as either explorers reporting back on strange lands or missionaries bringing civilisation to the 'great unwashed'. These remain very powerful traits in this field.

A good example is Jones' (2011) discussion of the reporting of the Matthews case at the beginning of *Chavs*. Karen Matthews hatched a bizarre plot to fake the kidnap of her daughter who she then reported as missing. As the plot unravelled, the great and good of metropolitan journalism descended on the impoverished estate in Dewsbury where the Matthews lived. As Jones notes, these largely university (many Oxbridge) educated, affluent reporters had been sent to an alien land where they struggled to understand local customs. The result was a series of articles that claimed to offer the reader an insight in to a corner of allegedly 'hidden' Britain.

Stedman-Jones (2013) concluded that the notion of the residuum began to disappear as economic growth at the turn of the century began to create employment. Social Darwinism and eugenics were strong features in debates about the social problem of the poor in the early part of the 20th century, and although the horrors of Nazism meant that support for eugenics disappeared from polite discourse, it is a recurring feature of Right-wing responses to these issues. As late as 1974, one of the intellectual gurus of Thatcherism, Sir Keith Joseph, ended hopes of further political advancement and leadership of the Tory Party when he stated that our 'human stock is threatened' – because too many poor mothers have children. Despite the advances of the post-war welfare state, concerns remained about a small group of families that seemed to be immune or unable to benefit from increased social provisions (Welshman, 2013). In the 1950s, the term 'problem families' was used for this group. The themes in the identification of the so-called 'problem families' appear as subtle variations of those identified in earlier periods, casting poverty as an individual or family rather than a structural issue. Worklessness and/or alcohol or drug abuse are seen as important factors. Alongside this analysis two major concerns are identified – that such families consume far too many state resources, and that they have too many children.

The cyclical nature of capitalism has meant that these concerns move to and fro within political and social policy debates. Social and political crises either lead to the state to examine its fiscal position or there are broader concerns about the nature of society. In both scenarios the role of the welfare state is questioned. In the first scenario, a fiscal crisis is used as justification for cuts, an argument that resurfaced with the introduction of austerity policies. In the second scenario, the welfare state – or, more accurately, benefits paid to the poorest – is seen as creating a morally corrupting culture of dependency. Within these discourses the broader social benefits of progressive welfare policies are washed away in the concentration on a small unrepresentative sample of recipients. There are elements of this in Lewis' (1969) culture of poverty thesis that argued that those living in poverty develop social habits and attitudes that make it difficult or impossible for individuals to escape their situation. In the 1970s, critics argued that cycles of deprivation explained the continued existence of poverty across generations. Sir Keith Joseph' speech, discussed above, was heavily influenced by this thesis. The argument here is that the roots of poverty are in individual family pathology. The emphasis is on individual and community failings rather than structural issues. These approaches are fundamentally pessimistic. One of their basic premises is that any state interventions have failed and will fail – the individuals and families are too trapped in these anti-social cultures.

This forms the historical roots of the term the 'underclass'. There is a tendency within certainly the media, but perhaps also academic circles, to look for the appearance of new or radically different social phenomena. There are elements of this in the history of the term 'underclass'. Poor and marginalised people existed long before the Swedish economist Gunnar Myrdal's first use of the term in 1963, which defined the underclass as follows:

> … there is a tendency to trap an 'underclass' of unemployed and gradually unemployable persons and families at the bottom of society. (Myrdal, 1963, p 3)

This is a structural explanation, although one with fairly clear moral overtones. However, the more modern use of the term 'underclass' has seen it become a term of contempt, carrying with it a whole series of assumptions about the moral worth of the individuals who are ascribed this class position.

The underclass has become one of the most powerful phrases in the sociopolitical lexicon. Wacquant (2009a) outlines the ways in which academics in alliance with think-tanks and sympathetic journalists seek to shape and mould debates in these areas. Welshman (2013) demonstrates the importance of individuals, for example, in the 1890s by Booth. In the case of the spread of the term 'underclass' in its current usage, the key individual is undoubtedly the American academic Charles Murray. The widespread usage of the term and the way that it has influenced policy is testimony to its power and influence. The rise of Murray and the term 'the underclass' can almost be viewed as a case study in the nexus of academia, think-tanks and journalism that Wacquant criticises so powerfully.

Murray is a libertarian American political social scientist. He became more widely known for his work, *Losing ground: American social policy 1950–1980* (1994). In this work, he set out a libertarian critique of American social policy of the 30 year period 1950–1980 . Murray argues that social welfare programmes are bound to fail and end up harming those members of society that they are designed to help. Murray has become an increasingly controversial figure. In *The bell curve: Intelligence and class structure in American life* (Herrnstein and Murray, 1994), he puts forward an essentially racist argument that differences in social outcomes – especially for African Americans – are linked to differences in IQ. In his latest book published in 2012, *Coming apart: The state of White America, 1960-2010*, Murray argues that differences in IQ and genetic make-up explain the divisions that have occurred within US society. Murray's work has been attacked not simply because of its ideological underpinning – the methodology that he and Herrnstein use to reach their conclusions in *The bell curve* has been widely disparaged. Despite this, Murray has been lauded by the American political establishment – including Republicans and Democrats.

Murray's work has become increasingly influential over that past 20 years. The 'doxa' of the underclass debate – that such a class exists, that it was created by the dependency of an over-generous welfare state and that its members live by a different moral standard to the wider community – have become very well established in political and public discourses. The link between academia, think-tanks and the media is illustrated by the journey Murray's work has made across the Atlantic. The linkage of welfare with dependency has moved from the work of academics such as Murray (1990) and Mead (1992) to the policy realm of government.

Murray's work was published by the Institute of Economic Affairs (IEA) and then taken up by *The Sunday Times* in the early 1990s. His work is a racialised discourse; in a clear form of Haney-Lopez's (2015) dog whistle politics, welfare becomes overwhelmingly associated with poverty in the African-American community. In considering Murray's arguments, it is important to note that in his analysis the underclass are not all those living in poverty. It represents a sub-stratum that are, in Murray's terms, socially, psychologically and culturally cut off from wider. The fact that his analysis sees the underclass as a totally separate group generates some of its divisive traction. For Murray, poverty is the result of individuals making poor social and lifestyle choices – women in this group have too many children, too early in their lives, fathered by irresponsible men. The key factor for Murray is that the welfare state allows individuals to make these choices. In addition, what he sees as a decline in social attitudes means that there is no longer any social stigma attached to illegitimacy. It is, perhaps, only in Murray's and his followers' work that the term even appears.

The term 'underclass' has been criticised for being a weak analytical concept (Wacquant, 2009b). The stigmatised representations of the poor – the welfare queen milking the system for huge sums of money – are discussed in more depth in Chapter 4. It is an imprecise value-laden term, one result being that it undermines the poor's claim to citizenship, or that it can become a strangely comforting notion for many. It provides an individualised explanation of poverty – the moral failings of those in this group. However, to highlight its sociological weaknesses is only part of the process. Murray and others have largely set the terms for recent debates about poverty, welfare and public policy. It is possible to argue that his work has been as influential on progressive parties as it has on those of the Right. In the US, Clinton's pledge to 'end welfare as we know it' and subsequent policies to implement it are imbued with rhetoric influenced by Murray's key notions.

In the UK context, as the state has withdrawn from a programme of social welfare provision, those systems that remain have become increasingly punitive (Crossley, 2015). This shift is very apparent in the British context, and has continued whatever the political complexion of recent governments. Barr et al's (2015) study of the recently introduced system of work capability assessments (WCAs) for those in receipt of disability benefits highlights negative impacts on the mental health of those subject to this new regime. The authors argue that the effects included an additional 590 suicides and nearly three-quarters of a million more prescriptions for anti-depressants. The early achievements of the Blair government in reducing child poverty and investing in public services have been lost (Toynbee and Walker, 2011), as despite positive investments in services such as Sure Start, the Blair years also saw the return of a more judgemental discourse around the causes of poverty and appropriate policy responses (Butler and Drakeford, 2001).

This tone was continued under the coalition government from 2010 onwards. In 2011, a series of riots began in London and then spread across other urban areas. The punitive trend in social policy became more pronounced after these riots. The government's social policy response was the Troubled Families Agenda, which has its origins in the New Labour government's 2006 Respect Agenda that claimed to identify a group of chaotic families who were a drain on public services, including health, social services, education and the police. As Crossley (2015) notes, the Respect Agenda was, at least nominally, focused on multiple disadvantages such as low income and poor housing. In this new incarnation, 'troubled families' are described as:

... households who: are involved in crime and anti-social behaviour, have children not in school, have an adult on out of work benefits and cause high costs to the public purse. (Crossley, 2015a, p 264)

A clear rhetorical shift is evident. Levitas (2012) outlines the porous nature of these categories: a 'family with troubles' quickly becomes a 'troubled family'. Beddoe (2014) notes in her discussion of similar policy developments in New Zealand that these shifts have taken place at a time of cuts and retrenchment in the welfare budget. They therefore become part of an ideological discourse that justifies austerity, helping to create a poisonous public environment where the poorest members of society are demonised as 'feckless scroungers'.

Loïc Wacquant: A brief introduction

One of the most influential analyses of the broader social impacts of neoliberalism can be found in the works of Loïc Wacquant. Professor Wacquant was born in Montpelier in France in 1960. He was educated in France before completing a PhD in Chicago in 1994. As part of his military service, he completed a period of research in the French colony of New Caledonia. He is currently Professor of Sociology at the University of California at Berkeley, USA. To describe Professor Wacquant as prolific does not really do justice to the extent, quality and challenging nature of his work. He is renowned as a dynamic and engaging public speaker and lecturer. His articles have appeared in a wide range of journals including those in the fields of sociology, criminology, social anthropology and urban and cultural studies. In addition, he has published a number of highly influential books, the most notable of which are *Les prisons de la misère* (1999, translated into 20 languages; new and expanded English edition, *Prisons of poverty*, 2009a), *Body and soul: Ethnographic notebooks of an apprentice boxer* (2004), *Urban outcasts: A comparative sociology of advanced marginality* (2008b), and *Punishing the poor: The neoliberal government of social insecurity* (2009b). These works form the core of Wacquant's work on welfare and penal policy. It can be divided into three key areas: advanced marginality, race (ethnoracial domination) and the rise of the penal state.

Wacquant (2012) argues that the analysis of neoliberalism can be characterised by two very broad approaches. The first is tied to an essentially economic model that examines the impact of the application of the 'market' to an area of public and private life previously seen as 'social goods' or 'beyond the market'. Harvey (2005) has described this process as 'accumulation by dispossession'. The second is derived from Foucault's notion of governmentality and examines how power is decentralised in late modern capitalist society. Foucault (2008) examines the construction of the modern discourse of citizenship with its emphasis on self-government and regulation. Wacquant (2012) argues that these two approaches 'obscure what is neo about neoliberalism'. He uses Bourdieu's notion of the bureaucratic field as his main analytical tool for his dissection of the development of the 'neoliberal Leviathan'. For Wacquant, the application of the notion of the bureaucratic field results in the identification of three key features of the neoliberal state. He argues that neoliberalism cannot be viewed solely as an economic project. It is a political one that inevitably involves the dismantling of welfare provisions. Welfare systems are replaced by 'workfare' or 'prisonfare' as a means of regulating marginal urban populations. As part of this process the balance between what Bourdieu termed the left hand and right hand of the state tilts. Wacquant describes this as a shift from 'the protective (feminine and collectivising) pole to the disciplinary (masculine and individualising) of the bureaucratic field' (Wacquant, 2012, p 73). This shifts necessarily involves an expansion of the penal state.

In his great trilogy of studies of *Urban outcasts* (2008b), *Punishing the poor* (2009b) and *Prisons of poverty* (2009a), Wacquant outlines the impact of the economic prospects of marginalised urban communities of the US and France. His analysis highlights the long-term impacts of the decline in skilled, unionised work. Wilson's *When work disappears* (1996) and *The truly disadvantaged* (2012) outlined the impact on communities and family structure of the initial phases of the neoliberal restructuring of economies that took place from the mid-1970s onwards. In this process, the economic and social security provided by Fordism was removed. Giroux (2011) argues that the impact of neoliberalism is to shrink the realm of democratic politics as the market pushes these values to the margin. Bauman (2008) suggests that the result is to create a world of 'hyper-individualism', where a sense of community or obligation to others begins to disappear.

Social practitioners are trying to balance the key values of social justice with a practice environment that seems at odds with these beliefs (Featherstone et al, 2014; Garrett, 2014; Webber et al, 2014). In addition, social work has increasingly found itself responding to an agenda that recasts the problems of poverty and social deprivation as individual lifestyle choices (Casey, 2016). Wacquant, following on from Bourdieu, provides a clear theoretical framework to explain and challenge these developments. His analysis of neoliberalism as a distinct political project that brings with it a new form of statecraft provides a starting point for a social work practice response to increasing inequality in modern societies. Wacquant's work focuses on the developing structures of inequality. In this analysis, inequalities are not simply economic; they are spatial and psychological. His theorisation provides a way of exploring the pressures and fissures within urban marginalised communities, recognising that there are community groups and activists working to combat these issues, while identifying the structural barriers that these efforts are confronted with.

Advanced marginality

The use of 'advanced marginality' as a term is an attempt to capture the mechanisms by which a sizable proportion of urban populations are excluded from or cut off from the ladders of social mobility in modern society. It captures the notion that within modern capitalism, poverty is spatially and (racially) concentrated. In advanced capital societies, these processes and systems would include access to decent housing, healthcare, education, well paid and secure employment and safe neighbourhoods. This analysis is of vital importance to social work as it acknowledges the impact lack of opportunity has on those who experience these forms of social exclusion. Kelly (2005), in his analysis of societal responses to mental illness, used the term 'structural violence' adopted from liberation theology as a means of exploring the intersections between mental health status, poverty, racism and discrimination. There are overlaps between that use and the term 'advanced marginality'. It is a counterpoint to the pathologising quasi-eugenic analysis that sprang from the underclass discourse outlined above. It recognises the complex interaction between agency and structure, emphasising that it is impossible to provide an analysis that does not acknowledge both.

In *Urban outcasts* (2008b), Wacquant produces a comparative analysis of two urban environments – the housing projects of Chicago and the banlieue (suburbs) of France. He argues that there are significant differences in the way that the marginalisation of poorer groups occurs in the post-Fordist metropolis, that the marginalisation that neoliberalism has produced is not a temporary feature. Rather, it is an endogenous feature brought about by the ways in which new forms of precarious employment and the removal of the social state have created new social structures. One of the key features of neoliberalism has been the increase in inequality and social polarisation. As part of this process, there has been a spatial concentration of poverty.

Alongside these developments, a stigmatising discourse of terms has entered the public domain. These are terms such as inner city, ghettos, no-go areas, enclaves and sink estates. Bourdieu's work in exploring the importance of symbolic power is important in these processes. Wacquant (2008b, 2009a, 2009b) argues that the state has taken on a key role in classification and stratification. In these processes, the neoliberal state is strangely both present and yet absent in the lives of many marginalised citizens. It is present in its authoritarian or punitive forms – the expansion of the penal state, discussed in Chapter 4, being the most obvious example. However, the retrenchment of the welfare regimes has seen the role of the state in the provision of services designed to improve the quality of life of citizens greatly diminished.

Territorial stigmatisation

Wacquant (2007) argues that 'territorial stigmatisation' – the processes whereby areas are characterised by:

> ... forms of poverty that are neither residual, nor cyclical or transitional, but inscribed in the future of contemporary societies insofar as they are fed by the ongoing fragmentation of the wage labour relationship, the functional disconnection of dispossessed neighbourhoods from the national and global economies, and the reconfiguration of the welfare state in the polarizing city. (pp 66-7)

McKenzie (2015) applies this analytical lens to the day-to-day lives of residents on an estate in Nottingham. She illustrates the way that the wider society stigmatises individuals, families and communities simply because they live in the St Ann's area of Nottingham. Being a resident meant that one had to negotiate a series of deeply entrenched wider social attitudes. As she demonstrates, there is also strength and resilience in the community – capacities that are often ignored or pathologised outside of it. From the late 1990s onwards, in the UK and across Europe, there has been an ongoing moral panic (Cohen, 2011) about the 'ghettoisation' of socially deprived urban areas. The term 'ghetto' – in modern usage suggests an area of poor housing, poverty, substance misuse problems, high crime and gang violence. It also has racist overtones. In Drake and Cayton's classic (1993) study, the ghetto is described as a 'black city within the white'. Slater (2009) argues that the ghetto is a social and psychological space with its boundaries created by ethnicity. However, it is also a space that sustains social ties and generates community organisation.

In Wacquant's schema, there are significant structural and cultural differences between modern, urban, spatially concentrated poverty and the 'ghetto', as understood in the above analysis. Wacquant proposes that social and community institutions are much more difficult to develop in contemporary environments. Previously strong civic institutions, ranging from the political to the social, and from trade unions to sports and youth clubs, have either been lost or are struggling to survive in the current precarious neoliberal world. The lack of social, educational and cultural amenities adds to the experience of poverty.

Wacquant (2010) argues that the underclass discourse not only corrodes the sense of self of those living in the poorest areas, but also makes it more difficult to develop and maintain broader social relationships. These are vital as they can act as supports for individuals and provide a buffer against the pressure that the insecure nature of much modern employment creates. It is important to note that Wacquant is not suggesting that such social systems do not exist. For example, in *Body and soul* (2004), he examines the experience of young black men who use a gym in Chicago, and considers the function of these informal structures in some detail. In a similar vein, McKenzie (2015) focuses not only on the economic and social pressures facing residents, but also the ways in which they overcome them.

Modern representation of poverty and stigma

In this section, I examine the impact of stigma and its links with modern representations of poverty. In the modern media-saturated world, the significance and importance of representation cannot be underestimated. As we have seen, there are continuities between Victorian representations of the poorest areas of cities and the underclass discourse. In both, the poorest areas are seen as urban hells, the source of criminality, dirt and disease.

The starting point for this discussion is Goffman's (1963) work on stigma; there then follows an analysis of modern representations of poverty. I use Jensen and Tyler's (2015) work to explore the ways in which the media – particularly tabloid newspapers and reality TV (RTV) – have helped shape an 'anti-welfare commonsense'. Hall (1997) argued that mass media has a crucial role in defining issues and influencing what become matters of public concern; Hall was writing at a time before the development of social media. It is clear that mainstream and social media are now in a symbiotic relationship.

Hall's analysis of the media representation of Black Britons remains very pertinent, but could also easily be applied to other groups. He notes that it is only when they are associated with a 'social problem' or issue that black Britons become visible to the mainstream media. The daily reality and complexity of individual and community lives struggles to find its way into the daily news cycle.

The day-to-day reality of those living in poverty is often reduced, in mainstream media, to a parade of stereotypes and media-created 'grotesques'.

Goffman (1963, p 3) describes stigma as an 'attribute that is deeply disturbing', and goes on to suggest that this attribute reduces the holder 'from a whole and usual to a discounted one.' There has been a significant expansion in the use of stigma as an analytical tool. It is widely applied to an analysis of personal circumstances in relation to physical disability, race, sexual orientation and mental health. Stigma can thus be seen as characteristic of groups or individuals who are deemed to be, in some way, outside the norms of broader society. This results in the construction of categories, what Foucault (1982) termed 'dividing practices', which are also linked to sets of stereotypical beliefs. As Link and Phelan (2001) argue, stigmatisation is inevitably entwined with social, economic and political power and capital. The labelling of individuals and the construction of stereotypes is followed by disapproval, rejection and discrimination. Goffman suggested that those who are stigmatised – he termed these the 'socially defeated' – remain connected to the 'socially thriving'. He concluded that 'the dead are sorted out but not segregated and continue to walk among the living.' Goffman also noted that the stratification of society almost inevitably involved the creation of an idolised view of its upper reaches.

Dorling et al (2007) noted that before the economic crisis in 2008, the gap in inequality had been at its widest for 40 years. As inequality has increased so the representation of those who are in the poorest group has become more hostile. An analysis of stigma related to class position has to include popular culture and representations of marginalisation. Inequality is not a simply a matter of economic position; it is concerned with cultural and symbolic representation. Class relationships and identities are dynamic, not static. Individuals can embrace but also reject them as well as create varieties of them. Lockyer's (2010) examination of the way that class operates in comedies emphasises the central nature of class relationships in British television. Within this framework, the poor and socially marginalised have increasingly become a target of a more vicious and less sympathetic comedy.

This trend was epitomised by the figure of the teenage single mother, Vicky Pollard, one of the most successful characters from the sketch show 'Little Britain' (BBC, 2003-08). Vicky Pollard's character – the creation of two male, privately educated, comedians – came to be seen as the archetype of the promiscuous single mother living off the welfare state. Pollard is a grotesque figure (Bakhtin, 1984), ridiculed for her stupidity and vulgarity. Skeggs (2005) notes that working-class female sexuality has often been presented as problematic. This is based on an assumption that middle-class feminine notions of decorum and restraint are rejected. Vicky Pollard was one of the most popular figures on the show. She was soon being referred to in news reports and so on as if she was a real figure, and used as shorthand for the failings of welfare policy. 'Little Britain' is inviting, or more accurately, demanding, that we laugh at a figure who has no redeeming features or characteristics. Some might argue that this is overestimating the importance of a character on a sketch show. Others will argue they are 'just joking', defending themselves with a phrase that Goffman described as being one of the most commonly used in the English language (Goffman, 1974). The 'joke' reflects broader class dynamics – the poor are being held up to ridicule for wider entertainment.

Anti-welfarism

Tyler (2008) outlines the dynamics of new forms of classism. As she notes, these amount to a form of class disgust. The development and trajectory of this disgust can be outlined in the consideration of the term 'chav'. It was the Oxford English Dictionary (OED) word of the year in 2004, often said to be an acronym for 'council-housed and violent'. It has tremendous cultural and social traction. The OED defines the term as an informal derogatory British term for 'a young lower-class person who displays brash and loutish behaviour and wears real or imitation designer clothes.' This does not quite capture the strength of the term, particularly the way that it is encapsulates a sense of disgust. Tyler argues that the emergence of the figure of the 'chav' in popular discourse indicates the shift in class relations. The term managed to combine a series of earlier popular, older stereotypes of the poor – the welfare scrounger, the petty criminal and the football hooligan. One of the ironies of this process was that the figure of the chav was associated with excessive consumerism – the focus on designer clothing brands and so on – which is surely one of the key cultural tropes of neoliberalism. Bourdieu's (2010) notion of capital emphasised the importance of the cultural sphere as a marker of social position but also as a barrier or border. In this schema, taste is a way of signifying membership of a group, but also excluding those seen as undesirable. Nayak (2003) shows that there are similarities between the ways in which racist groups represent immigrants and the representation of the poor. These coalesce around the figure of the chav. Prominence is given to metaphors of disease, with 'The other' represented as an invading army. As discussed below, there is a fixation with excessive breeding, based on a fear that it will dilute or weaken the nationalist gene pool.

Reactions of disgust reveal wider social dynamics and power relations. Skeggs (2005) notes that class as a tool and site of analysis was on the wane at a time when inequality in British society reached new heights – or perhaps, more accurately, depths. The use of terms such as 'inequality' or 'social exclusion' was part of this process. The problems of poverty are thus presented as technical issues rather than structural or moral ones. Ehrenreich (1990) noted the faltering progress on the issues of race and sexuality where the direction of travel appeared progressive and did not include class. Class remained steeped in prejudice. The post-Brexit atmosphere in the UK and the toxic US presidential election appears to place progress on these issues in doubt. The public discourse has certainly become more toxic.

Jensen and Tyler (2015, p 471) outline the development a new form of political economy where they identify what they term a 'hardening anti-welfare commonsense'. They use the reporting of the case of Mick Philpott who was convicted alongside his wife Mairead for the manslaughter of six of his children in an arson attack at their home. Philpott had actually appeared on other RTV programmes that claim to portray the reality of life on benefits. This genre of RTV, termed 'poverty porn', includes programmes such as 'Benefit Street' that present a series of stereotyped and negative images of the poor to the rest of the nation. Jensen and Tyler argue that such programmes, alongside the tabloid reporting of the welfare system, have had a vital role in the creation of a climate of hostility towards the very institution of the welfare state. These debates take the work of Murray as their starting point in such a fashion that the issue to be solved is not poverty, but welfare dependency (Peck and Theodore, 2010).

As noted above, one recurring theme in the discussion of the welfare state is the idea that it is so generous that it allows excessive breeding among the poor. Jensen and Tyler (2015) argue that the 'benefits brood' family is one of the key figures in this mythology. Politicians and the tabloid press used the Philpott case to claim that it demonstrated the need for austerity policies and a reduction in welfare. As with Shannon Matthews in *Chavs*, Philpott was somehow seen to be representative of all those on welfare. It should be noted that both were extraordinary cases, involving the commission of serious crime by individuals who can hardly be regarded, in any sense, as representative of those on welfare. Philpott, the father of 17 children, planned an arson attack that resulted in the death of six of his children. Yet he was portrayed in the tabloid press as the product of a bloated welfare state. The welfare state has been in a state of crisis since the early 1970s, and this crisis is seen through one of two lenses – the creation of dependency or a government fiscal crisis that is used for justification for retrenchment (Langan, 1998). In their analysis of the reporting of the Philpott case, Jensen and Tyler (2015) show the key role that the 'benefits brood' has in generating anti-welfare commonsense. The repeated appearances of the same families – Philpott had appeared on several such shows – gives the impression that there are many more such families than actually exist. In response to a Freedom of Information request from *The Sun* in 2012, the Department for Work and Pensions revealed that there were 10 families dependent on benefits where there were 13 or more children.

Conclusion

Sociologists such as Wacquant have used the insights of Goffman as a starting point from which to explore the impact of the psychosocial impacts of poverty. Scheff (2003) notes that shame is part of a large family of emotions, but also that it is a very powerful and corrosive one. Chase and Walker (2013) argue that shame is, in some senses, co-produced. In 2014/15, The Trussell Trust reported that over a million people had accessed a food bank. Garthwaite (2016a) reports that despite their widespread use, there is still a stigma attached to them. Users reported to her that they felt stigma not because of the way that they were treated at the food bank – as one might expect, those who attended food banks reported that the staff treated them with dignity and respect. The main reasons for using food banks were factors that many would see as out of the control of the individuals – benefit sanctions policies, delays in payments, low pay and insecure work. However, stigmatising attitudes were the result of how people thought that they would be seen, not only by the wider community, but also themselves. There is an interplay here between cultural attitudes, media representation and individuals, and it is this complex interplay that generates and sustains stigma.

FOUR

Welfare, punishment and neoliberalism

This chapter considers the broader impact of neoliberalism on welfare and penal policy. The main thrust of the argument here is that there has been an ideological and culture shift, which can be summarised as follows: the War on Poverty to a War on the Poor. The main thrust of the argument here is that as the state has withdrawn from a programme of social welfare provision, state systems and responses to poverty have become increasingly punitive in their outlook and approach. In the UK, this general trend is discernible from the mid-1970s onwards.

There was a brief hiatus under the first Blair Labour government. However, this period of investment in public services stands out against the trend, with the shift accelerating after the riots in 2011. There were two clear themes in the Blairite approach to welfare – an investment in education and health, although this investment was accompanied by a more moralistic discourse. The early achievements of the Blair years in tackling poverty and investing in public services have been lost. Alongside the positive investment in services such as Sure Start, the return of a more moralistic discourse around the causes of poverty and appropriate policy responses was evident. This tone continued under the coalition government.

Garland (2014) notes that intellectuals such as Beveridge, Marshall and Titmuss, behind the development of modern social protection systems in the UK, were opposed to the use of the term 'welfare state'. They recognised that then, as now, its opponents use it pejoratively. The modern state has many, sometimes contradictory, functions. All modern developed states are welfare states in the sense that there exist forms of social insurance, education and healthcare, which are in some ways the responsibility of government. However, the dominance of the neoliberal discourse has meant that the term 'welfare state' has come to be only associated with government relief for the poor (Garland, 2014). This obscures not only the true functions and role of social protection, but also the broader role of the state. Hills (2015) demonstrates that the nature of welfare is much more complex than these debates allow. They also obscure which groups benefit from state welfare, and the mechanisms underpinning this.

Piven and Cloward (2012), in their classic book, argue that the role of welfare has always been twofold – to ensure the maintenance of civil order and to control the labour supply when markets are out of kilter. In this model, welfare provision becomes cyclical. The New Deal, the post-Second World War establishment of the modern British welfare state and Lyndon Johnson's War on Poverty in the 1960s are examples of 'political responses to political disorder'. Rodger (2008) argues that there has been an increasingly punitive approach to welfare. It is important to note here that welfare systems and the criminal justice system cannot be viewed in isolation from each other. Hinton (2016) shows in the US context that the roots of mass incarceration can be traced not only to the centuries of the demonisation of black men, but also to Johnson's War on Poverty. The rhetoric and assumptions of Johnson's welfare policies were replete with assumptions about African-American criminality. Therefore, Johnson, as well as calling for a War on Poverty, called for a War on Crime. This has echoes in the New Labour social and criminal justice system policies of the late 1990s – tough on crime, tough on the causes of the crime. As well as an increased investment in public services, the moralising tone of the New Labour project assumed that there was a small group of the poor who required greater state intervention. This could be seen in the development of workfare policies and also in the greater use of the criminal justice system. This chapter outlines the results, including a doubling of the prison population in a 20-year period.

Simon (2007) argues that the period of mass incarceration is a new form of statecraft. The main thrust of his argument is that new civil and political structures have developed. He terms this process governing through crime and argues that it is fundamentally different to the process of managing criminal behaviour that all states have to undertake. For Simon, the roots of governing through crime lie in the economic and political crises of the 1970s and 1980s. Failure to manage the economic crisis led to a crisis in government legitimacy. The politicalisation of the law and order question was a feature of the elections that returned neoliberal governments in the US and UK throughout the 1980s. Simon argues that the victim of crime, particularly violent crime, came to act as the dominant model of citizenship. He provides several examples where violent crime has had a direct impact on the election process, the most famous of these being the case of Willie Horton, a convicted murderer, who raped a woman while he was on a period of weekend leave. George Bush (Senior) used this case in an attack advert on Dukakis in the 1988 presidential campaign. This approach has become a dominant governmental meme, spilling over into other areas of social policy such as mental health. Cummins (2012) demonstrates the ways in which the responses to the failings of community care recast mental health policy in terms of an issue of law and order rather than social welfare.

Models of welfare

In his 1990 work, *The three worlds of welfare capitalism*, Esping-Andersen produced a highly influential typology of welfare states.

- Liberal welfare states: welfare provision is largely privatised – public provision is at a low level and its use is highly stigmatised
- Conservative/corporatist welfare states: strong emphasis on supporting traditional values and family structures with a focus on, for example, child/family payments
- Social democratic welfare states: mostly closely associated with modern Swedish welfare state – high quality public services funded by high personal taxation push out private provision

The UK welfare system is a usually regarded as an uneasy hybrid, although it most closely resembles the liberal model, with universal provision provided by the NHS standing out. There is not the space to debate the validity and utility of Esping-Andersen's typology in detail here, but it establishes that all states are involved in these areas, and the debate is about the nature and structure of that provision. In addition, it should be emphasised that the typology is based on ideal types, and there will be local and national variations – the US has different provisions in each state, for example. Hawaii introduced legislation in 1974 that means that employers have to offer healthcare insurance to employees working 20 or more hours a week. The result is that it has one of the highest rates of medical insurance coverage.

It is important that we approach these models with some caution as they can obscure the disparities or abuses within welfare systems. For example, the Swedish welfare state is often held up as a model of generosity and inclusivity. However, in 1997, the leading Swedish newspaper, *Dagens Nyheter*, revealed that Swedish governments had followed a policy of compulsory sterilisation of adults with learning difficulties between 1935 and 1975.

For Peck and Tickell (2002), neoliberalism is a dominant and almost universal ideology that is difficult to escape. They summarise its main features as follows:

> The new religion of neoliberalism combines a commitment to the extension of markets and logics of competitiveness with a profound antipathy to all kinds of Keynesian and/ or collectivist strategies. The constitution and extension of competitive forces is married with aggressive forms of state downsizing, austerity financing, and public- service "reform". (p 381)

In this model, the market and the state are in opposition or even in competition. This is a misleading binary as the state plays a key role in markets (Chang, 2011, 2014) in terms of investment, infrastructure and supporting research and development. In addition, as the result of neoliberal influences, the state is increasingly marketised (Hutton, 1995).

The neoliberal argument against welfare systems is twofold – they are expensive and create dependency. The expansion of the so-called 'Washington consensus' via bodies such as the World Trade Organisation and The World Bank has seen increasing pressure on national modes of welfare provision. The argument here is that the hyper-mobility of capital marginalises national government that has to lower taxes and weaken employees' rights to continue to attract investment. Globalisation was seen as signalling the end of the European welfare model based on high taxation and investment in social goods (Beck, 1999). The forces of globalisation, or more accurately, neoliberalism, place tremendous pressures on welfare provision (Yeates, 2002). There is a danger of assuming that all welfare provision is now based on a liberal US model. Esping-Andersen (1996) and Gough (2000) argue that there is still a diversity of welfare state provision. The experiences of poverty and state support offered to those in need are still very different across jurisdictions. The devolution and decentralisation of some of these functions mean that they are very different within in the UK – student tuition fees being an obvious example.

In Chapter 2, I outlined the increase in inequality that has been the result of neoliberal-influenced policies. Esping-Andersen (2002) sees the creation of a 'new welfare architecture' as one result of these shifts. He identifies a more polarised society where there are clear divisions between what he terms low-income/work-poor families and resource-strong/work-rich families. Within this society, the role of the state has become much more focused on ensuring that adults are responsible parents and citizens capable of meeting the demands of the modern workplace (Hansen and Stepputat, 2001). These processes have always existed, but were balanced by moves to meet social and individual needs. Social work as a profession developed in this social space. Donzelot (1979) argues that the creation of this social space – between the individual, family and wider society – was the result of public interest in the governance of the pathologised urban poor. Welfare states have always been exclusionary in that they are based on a notion of universal citizenship where that citizen is an able-bodied white man. Citizenship is a highly contested notion (Lister, 1997). Nation, people and race become one, thus denying even the existence of Black Britishness (Gilroy, 2002). Alongside this is a parallel but strangely incoherent dual narrative that immigrants are attracted to the country because of generous benefits, but are, at the same time, taking jobs from British workers. The ways in which these welfare systems are racialised and gendered are not made explicit. The work of Emejulu and Bassel (2015) shows that these processes continue – with the impact of austerity falling disproportionately on 'women of colour'.

Progressive parties in the US and Europe faced a significant challenge at the end of the 1990s. They had been out of power for a decade or more, but changes in the economy also meant that their traditional power bases – unionised labour and progressive middle-class professionals – had been fractured and weakened. The Clinton Democrats in the US and New Labour in the UK reached the conclusion that to be re-elected they would need to appeal to a new coalition. Socially progressive liberalism in the areas of equality was to be coupled with a strong commitment to tackling the issues of crime and social responsibility. Wacquant has noted that the doxa of neoliberalism have become increasingly powerful. In the area of social policy, the key themes were modernisation and reform. This so-called 'Third Way' (Giddens, 1998) presented itself as an escape from the dogmas of the past. New Labour felt that it was seen as 'on the side' of the poor – and in case of any doubt, this was a bad thing and a political liability – Labour had to be seen as siding with middle-class and upper-working-class voters – or, in the awful language of the time, 'the aspirational'.

I am writing this chapter on the day after MPs have rejected a motion that stated that Blair misled the House of Commons in the run-up to the Iraq War. I mention this as it is in such stark contrast to the early triumphs of his political career. These include winning three general elections and also a period when he was undoubtedly the dominant political figure of his time. In 1997, New Labour won a landslide victory with a huge overall majority of 179. Labour actually won 418 seats and made a net gain of 145 (see www.ukpolitical.info/1997. htm). Blair made it clear that he would govern as a New Labour.

This represented a shift from previous Labour government. In the area of welfare, the early period saw the continuation of moves away from a Keynesian welfare model to the development of a workfare approach (Roger, 2000; Jessop, 2002). The model of welfare pursued has been termed a social investment state. As a politician, Blair was heavily influenced by the ideas of the communitarian philosopher Amitai Etzioni. Communitarianism is best understood as a reaction to the modern exposition of liberalism that is found in Rawls. In *A theory of justice* (Rawls, 1971), Rawls argued that a concept of justice must be based on the rights of individuals, as 'each person possesses an inviolability founded on justice that even the welfare of society as a whole cannot override' (1971, p 3). Communitarians argue that this conception of liberal individualism overlooks the fact that individuals live in communities. Sandel (2009, p 220) summarises this criticism thus:

> ... the weakness of the liberal conception of freedom is
> bound up with its appeal. If we understand ourselves as free
> and independent selves, unbound by moral ties we haven't
> chosen, we can't make sense of a range of moral and political
> obligations that we commonly recognize, even prize.

The New Labour approach to welfare thus has to be understood as partly motivated by the communitarian philosophy at its heart, but also a real political desire not to be seen as weak in this area. One can see some traditional Labour concerns – investment in education and the NHS – and also some concerns such as the need to prevent welfare dependency that represent a continuity with the Conservative governments that preceded it.

According to Olk (2006), changes in patterns of employment and social structures are reflected in broader attitudes to welfare. The division or cleavage is now cast not as one between rich and poor, but between insiders and outsiders. This is a reformulation of *The established and the outsiders* (Elias and Scotson, 1994), based on research that took place on a suburban housing estate in Leicester, which was given the name Winston Parva. Elias studied conflict between two actually very similar groups of residents on the estate. Elias developed a conceptual framework – established–outsider relations – to explain this conflict. Elias and Scotson argued that residents who had lived on the estate longer stigmatised newer residents for lacking the superior qualities that this group attributed to itself. The result was that slurs were cast on members of one group not because of their individual qualities, but because they were members of that group. A whole new political lexicon has been created since 1987 that tries to articulate these broad established/outsider relations – phrases such as 'Worcester Woman', hard-working families, strivers – these are examples of codes that politicians use for 'people like us' who will vote for them. The dog whistle nature of modern politics means that the racialised nature of some of these codes is not made explicit (Haney-Lopez, 2015).

Welfare and austerity

The outcome of the 2010 general election saw the first formal coalition government in the UK since the Second World War. David Cameron, as Prime Minister, argued that one of the reasons for the need for a coalition was the national fiscal emergency that the country faced as a result of the rise in national debt. This rise was attributed not to the funds provided to bail out the banks in 2008; it was, successfully it must be said, portrayed as a result of profligate spending by the previous Labour government. As outlined in Chapter 1, the government introduced a policy of retrenchment that came to be known as 'austerity'. Austerity inevitably has the greatest impact on those who are the most reliant on social and welfare services. There is now a significant literature that outlines the impact of these policies on the poorest sectors of society. The extent to which the coalition government's policies impacted on the most vulnerable was demonstrated by the Centre for Welfare Reform's report, *A fair society?*, published before the 2015 general election, which highlighted that 50 per cent of cuts fell in just two areas, which together make up only 25 per cent of government spending:

- benefits to be cut by 20%, most of which is for disabled people and people in poverty
- local government budgets to be cut by over 40%, most of which, 60%, is for social care (which will be cut by 33%).

They target the very groups, I would argue, that a decent society should protect:

- people in poverty (1 in 5 of us) bear 39% of all the cuts
- disabled people (1 in 13 of us) bear 29% of all the cuts
- people with severe disabilities (1 in 50 of us) bear 15% of all the cuts

Austerity, rather than a response to a fiscal emergency, was clearly a political project. It sought to complete the work of Thatcherism and the 'reform of the welfare state'. The parts of New Labour that had sought to tackle child poverty such as Sure Start Centres, Child Trust Funds and targets for reducing child poverty were immediately sidelined.

The impact of austerity's shredding of the social safety net is documented in *Hunger pains: Life inside Foodbank Britain* (Garthwaite, 2016b). This shows that families and individuals are subject to an increasingly harsh welfare regime where the use of sanctioning, that is, stopping benefits, has increased. As discussed in Chapter 3 the impacts of poverty are psychosocial as well as physical. There is a stigma attached to using a food bank. This is further illustrated by the processes of work capability assessments (WCAs). The Department for Work and Pensions (DWP) introduced WCAs in 2008, as an assessment process to determine whether an individual is eligible for Employment and Support Allowance (ESA). There are three possible outcomes; that the person is:

- fit for work
- unfit for work, but fit for pre-employment training
- fit for neither work nor training

The DWP sees this as part of a process that will help people 'off benefits and into work'. The whole scheme has been a controversial one. Atos won the original contract, but earlier this year, another company, Maximus took over. The management of these schemes thus becomes commodified.

Assessment processes like the WCA are essentially functional. It is difficult to convey the potential impact of major mental health conditions such as depression, which do not physically prevent someone from working but mean it is impossible for them to carry out their normal role. People with mental health problems face well-documented stigma in the workplace and job market. It is important that they are offered appropriate support and advice. However, the WCA has been seen as essentially punitive, with its main aim being to reduce public expenditure. In addition, there have been real concerns about the impact of the WCA on the mental health of those who have been subject to it.

Barr et al's (2015) analysis is the first study of the impact of the introduction of the WCA process. In the period 2010–13, just over a million people were reassessed using the WCA, 80 per cent of existing claimants. And this reassessment varied across the country, for example, 71 per cent of claimants were assessed in Wokingham compared to 88 per cent in Knowsley. The authors conclude that in those areas with higher rates of reassessment, there were greater increases in suicides, self-reported mental health problems and anti-depressant prescribing. Across England as a whole in 2010 to 2013, the WCA was associated with:

- 590 suicides
- 725,000 additional prescriptions for anti-depressants
- 279,000 additional cases of self-reported mental health problems

The authors put these figures into context as follows. They represent:

- 5% of the total number of suicides
- 5% of the total number of anti-depressant prescriptions
- 11% of self-reported mental health problems

As more disadvantaged socioeconomic groups are more likely to be in receipt of disability benefits, and thus to be assessed, the reassessment policy was associated with a greater increase in adverse mental health outcomes in more deprived areas.

These findings are consistent with other research that suggests a link between increasing mental illness and the austerity and welfare reforms of recent years. The WCA was introduced without any evidence of its potential impact. Neither have there been any plans to evaluate its impact. The WCA is, in effect, a huge experiment in public health policy, an experiment in which the subjects did not volunteer; in fact, they had to take part. This research emphasises that policies that are designed to reduce welfare spending have real consequences for the individuals who rely on social protection systems. Schemes such as the WCA move people on to other benefits, and not into employment.

Barr et al's (2015) conclusion is very clear. The negative impact of this kind of welfare reform outweighs any potential benefit to the public purse. Such policies may even result in increased expenditure in other areas. They do not tackle the fundamental issue of access to employment for people with disabilities. The authors conclude that although the explicit aim of welfare reform in the UK is to reduce 'dependency', it is likely that targeting people living in the most vulnerable conditions with policies that are harmful to their health will further marginalise already excluded groups, reducing, rather than increasing, their independence.

It seems that the welfare state has always faced some form of crisis or another. The origins of the modern welfare state lie in recognition of the limits of the market. Esping-Andersen (1990) underlines the importance of the ways in which some benefits and services were decommodified, that is, taken out of market relations. The welfare aspects of the state are thus a corrective mechanism to market failings. This was the core of the social democratic welfare systems that developed in the period 1945-79. There was an acceptance that the state needed to have a greater role in modern market economies. For example, it is in the interests of modern capitalism to have a highly educated workforce, and this is a social good that the market will not be able to deliver. Neoliberalism has a polar opposite view and account of these processes. The mechanisms of the market are distorted by a welfare state that produces social wage legislation that adds to labour costs and has to be funded by personal and corporate taxation. It is argued that this burden falls most on those who are least likely to use public services. In addition, the welfare state has found itself under attack for the creation of dependency. It has to be acknowledged that neoliberalism has been very successful in creating and sustaining modern notions of depictions of welfare that have a long and inglorious history (Welshman, 2013).

Over the past 30 years, as well as what one might call its traditional enemies, social welfare programmes have faced the additional threat of globalisation – or, more accurately, hyper-mobile global capital. The forces of global capital have led to a situation where it appears that economics rather than local or national politics dominate. Market forces have become new Gods that, it appears, national leaders will disobey at their peril. The market has come to be seen as the most efficient means for the allocation of goods and services – including social goods that were previously seen as standing outside of it. Global capital is now seen as more powerful than the nation-state, with the result that the heads of world-leading companies are more significant figures than democratically elected politicians. While recognising these important trends, it should be noted that individuals and communities are not totally swept away in these processes.

What, then, are the implications for what we term the 'welfare state'? There has been a significant change in the role of the state here. The expansion of the penal state is examined later in this chapter. In the UK, the period of austerity has crystallised trends that can be seen as developing under New Labour. The analyses of Simon (2007), Rodgers (2008) and Wacquant (2008a, 2009a, 2009b) of the shifts in social and penal policy have one key theme in common. Welfare has become an increasingly restrictive and disciplinary function, although it has always played such a role. Jones and Novak (1999) argued that neoliberalism has involved the 'retooling' of the state and its reconfiguration in the capital's interests. In the area of welfare, this has meant privatisation of welfare services and the increased use of conditionality. The introduction of austerity economic policies in the UK has crystallised these trends. The result has been a shredding of social provision with a consequent impact on the poorest and most vulnerable members of society.

Lipsky (1980), in his seminal work *Street level bureaucracy*, outlined the ways in which public officials navigate their way through organisational processes that often run counter to the expressed values of the profession. Social work practitioners are trying to balance the key values of social justice with a practice environment that seems at odds with these beliefs (Featherstone et al, 2014; Garrett, 2014; Webber et al, 2014). In addition, social work has increasingly found itself responding to an agenda that recasts the problems of poverty and social deprivation as individual lifestyle choices (Casey, 2016). These tensions have increased as the 'reforms' of the welfare state have the greatest impact on those who are most likely to be in contact with social workers.

The rise of the penal state

Social work, in the broadest sense of the term, has always been concerned with the criminal justice system. Probation officers, until the reforms led by Michael Howard (former Home Secretary), were trained alongside social workers. I completed a CQSW at the University of Liverpool in the mid-1980s, working alongside my future social work colleagues. The curriculum was virtually identical for both groups, apart from the fact that probation students completed a placement with a local probation team. Students were sponsored by the Home Office to undertake this training. The Probation Service described itself at that time as a 'social work agency within the criminal justice system'. The focus of the course was very much on sociological explanations of crime and offending. The Probation of Offenders Act 1907 had defined the role of the probation officer as to 'advise, assist and befriend' offenders. The whole ethos of the service at the time reflected this core purpose. Probation officers wrote court reports to assist judges and magistrates in sentencing, always looking for alternatives to custodial options. The focus of day-to-day probation work was a traditional casework model of practice supporting ex-offenders in finding employment, housing or tackling other issues such as alcohol or substance misuse. As Annison (2007) notes, there has been a huge shift in the training and role of probation officers. The current focus is very much on criminological approaches and risk, and risk management.

The criminal justice system has historically been one of the key sites of social work interventions. Throughout his work, Wacquant (2008b, 2009a and 2009b) has powerfully argued that the growth of social insecurity is one of the key features of neoliberalism. Insecurity is used in its broadest sense here to capture a transformed landscape, particularly in employment, where there are fewer well-paid long-term contracts with benefits and employment rights. Wacquant argues that the rise of the penal state is an endogenous feature of neoliberalism. As outlined below, this position is somewhat of an outlier. Penal and legal scholars such as Simon (2007), Harcourt (2011) and Drucker (2011) examine the expansion of the use of imprisonment via a broader cultural and policy lens. Wacquant uses the term 'doxa' to identify terms that construct but also limit the terms of policy debates. In the penal sphere, doxa would include phrases such as 'prison works', 'zero tolerance' and 'broken windows'. These terms, particularly in public discourse, are accepted in a largely uncritical fashion.

The increases in inequality outlined in Chapter 2, combined with a hardening of social attitudes, are the basis for the modern increase in punitive penal policies. And this punitive turn is not limited to penal policy. As Chapter 2 outlines, similar trends can be identified in the social and welfare policies since the crash of 2008. Wilkinson and Pickett (2009) argue that increased social inequality leads to reduced levels of social cohesion and community trust. More unequal societies are also more fractured ones. The 'othering' of other social groups – in this case, poor, marginalised, urban communities – is both a cause and an outcome of increased inequality. It is one of the key drivers of increased punitivism (Garland, 2004). Less contact between social groups makes for scapegoating and the production of feelings of alienation. The approach here is influenced by Bauman's (1989) analysis of the Holocaust. Modern approaches to punishment and broader penal policy create an image of the offender as an alien – someone who is 'not one of us'. This dehumanising process allows for such individuals to be treated with indifference or worse, contempt.

The expansion of the penal state has been most prominent in the US. In Europe, England and Wales have followed this upward curve most closely. It is important to acknowledge that penal policy is the result of the complex interaction of a range of social, cultural and historical factors. There are also distinct regional and even local differences. Any staff working in the criminal justice system will be aware that some courts or individual magistrates or judges will be seen as more punitive than others.

Imprisonment is an act of state violence inflicted on individuals, and has huge symbolic value and impact, which is not limited to the individual offender, but spreads outwards to families and communities. The expansion of the penal state – the increased use of imprisonment, the over-representation of those from racial minority ethnic groups, poor conditions and failure to address the needs of mentally ill prisoners – mean that penal policy must be an area that concerns all social workers.

'Governing through crime'

Changes in the training, roles and function of probation officers are a reflection of much broader shifts in cultural and social attitudes. Offenders who were once viewed as marginalised individuals in need of some form of welfare and social support are now seen in much more threatening terms. The focus is on risk, that is, what risk does an individual pose to the wider community? Will the offender do it again? This has been accompanied by a decline in a belief that offenders can be rehabilitated (Garland, 2001). One of the key arguments of this book is that these trends are not limited to the criminal justice system – they can be seen across social and welfare systems.

It is important to examine the social and political context in which criminal justice policy develops. The expansion of the use of imprisonment has been one of the most startling features of public policy over the past 25 years. This has occurred in a number of jurisdictions, most significantly in the US. Simon (2007) argues that the increase in the use of imprisonment is a reflection of wider social concerns about crime and personal safety. It is important to note here that Simon is not arguing that concerns about violent crime are somehow illegitimate; far from it. However, he identifies cultural trends that have amplified concerns with violent crime. These include an increased concern with personal safety; a focus on risk and risk management; responses such as gated communities; and a rise in the number of SUVs (Sport utility vehicles). These developments serve to create more disconnected atomised communities. Alongside these, there has been a forwarding of victims and victims' right within the criminal justice system. Individual high-profile cases also have a greater impact. In California, the brutal abduction and murder of Polly Klass in 1993 led to a campaign that resulted in the introduction of the 'three strikes law' in 1994, which sentences offenders who have been convicted of a third felony to life imprisonment.

Politicians from all political parties have responded to this trend by abandoning a traditional consensus that focused on rehabilitation. It should be noted that there has always been a strong populist authoritarian strain in these debates about crime and punishment. These issues crystallise around arguments about sentencing, prison conditions and the death penalty. Simon calls this meme and its impact on the political process 'governing through crime'. He argues that this is so deeply entrenched that progressive parties have been unable or unwilling to move the terms of the debate. The Clinton and Blair governments are both examples of this trend whereby progressive parties took a much harder line on law and order for fear that their political enemies would portray them as 'weak on crime'.

The penal state

Penal scholars have used a number of terms to describe the phenomenon of the increased use of penal sanctions. These include mass incarceration, mass imprisonment, the prison boom, the carceral state or the penal state. These terms refer to the phenomenon of the rise in the use of penal sanctions at a time when crime rates have been falling. Simon (2014) has compared this to a biblical flood, one that he now sees as past its peak. However, like all floods, it has created a tremendous amount of damage. In this case, the damage is to individuals, families and communities who have found themselves caught up in it.

The US has seen the greatest increase in the use of imprisonment. Such use in England and Wales has not, thankfully, grown in the same way, although it has doubled over a 20-year period where crime has generally been falling. There are three key elements to the ratcheting up of sentencing. The first is the creation of a climate of fear around crime. This has an impact on the political process, and community sentences are seen to lack validity or rigour. The second element sees the introduction of mandatory and/or indeterminate sentences. Finally there is a prison building programme. Once new prisons are built they are generally full. The standard rate of measure for imprisonment is the rate per 100,000 of the general population. This has increased worldwide from 136 to 144 per 100,000 since 1999. This total figure masks the significant differences between different jurisdictions in states and between countries themselves. The US has the highest incarceration rate in the world, at 716 citizens per 100,000. This overall rate hides huge racial and geographical disparities. Carson and Golinelli (2013) highlighted that the five states with the highest rates of imprisonment – Louisiana (1,720), Mississippi (1,370), Alabama (1,234), Oklahoma (1,178) and Texas (1,121) – had rates that were much higher than the national average.

In any society, those who are incarcerated come from the poorest, most marginalised groups. The impact of imprisonment is not restricted to the individuals serving a sentence. In the US context, scholars of the penal state have demonstrated the devastating impact on African-American communities – particularly urban ones (Mauer, 2006; Clear, 2009; Drucker, 2011). The social impacts of imprisonment do not end with the release of that individual. The stigma attached to imprisonment remains very powerful, and access to employment is a clear issue. However, as Alexander (2012) argues, there are other perhaps less well-known impacts. For example, in a number of states 'convicted felons' are denied the right to vote in all subsequent elections. There are also restrictions on accessing social housing and educational programmes. Alexander argues that this has created a 'caste' of disenfranchised young black men. The criminal justice system is thus managing but also reproducing societal inequalities.

Wacquant (2009a) argues that the US has played a pivotal role in the development of the penal state. Policies or approaches such as 'zero tolerance' and 'broken windows' have their roots in the US, and have been spread via a nexus of think-tanks and prominent individuals such as Bill Bratton, a former LAPD (Los Angeles Police Department) and NYPD (New York Police Department) Commissioner. Walmsley's (2015) analysis of patterns of imprisonment across the world shows that the prison as an institution is now more deeply embedded in social policy than ever before. There are currently approximately 10.2 million people in prison (see www.prisonstudies.org/world-prison-brief-data), nearly a quarter, 2.4 million, are in prison in the UK. The two other leading carceral nations, Russia (0.68 million) and China (1.64 million), alongside the US, hold nearly half the world's prisoners.

Locating penal policy

Comparisons between penal regimes cannot be made without a broader consideration of the wider cultural and political forces that influence their creation (Lacey, 2008). It is not that surprising that the US, with a deeply engrained cultural notion of individualism, sees crime very much in individual terms. Becker's (1968) Rational Choice Theory (RCT), in which offenders are making a rational choice to commit crime, is a prime example here. Possible punishment or other sanctions are part of a cost–benefit analysis that offenders make. This position has, in many areas, overtaken a more traditional welfare approach, which sees the roots of offending in personal as well as broader social conditions. Any examination of the expansion of imprisonment cannot be solely based on the penal policy. To use Bourdieu's terms, it has to consider the field and the habitus of the actors within it.

Cavadino and Dignan (2006), in their analysis of penal policies and the use of imprisonment, developed a political economy typology – neoliberal, conservative corporatist, social democratic and oriental corporatist. Examples of all these, apart from oriental corporatist, exist within Europe and the EU. Walmsley's (2015) most recent analysis of the use of imprisonment across the EU highlights the importance of this cultural factors approach. As might be expected, the Baltic States have the highest rates of imprisonment – these countries are still establishing the institutions of a civil society; as they become mature liberal democracies, one might expect these rates of imprisonment to fall.

There is a range of other national factors that need to be considered, such as Portugal's liberalisation of drug laws which has led to a reduction in the use of imprisonment. Germany and Holland are notable as countries where the use of imprisonment has fallen. Subramanian and Shames (2013) show that this is due to policies such as the concentrated use of community penalties and suspended sentences in both countries. The UK, Spain and France, however, are examples of countries where the use of imprisonment has been on an upward curve, and seems set to continue in that fashion. Downes and Hansen's (2016) analysis of 18 countries including the UK and US concluded that there was a clear relationship between welfare provision and penal policy: the lower the spending on welfare, the higher the rate of imprisonment.

There has been a great deal of debate in penal policy about the nature of Scandinavian exceptionalism, that is, their different approach to penal and welfare policy. The main features of these policies are low rates of imprisonment as well as different prison regimes that have rehabilitation at their heart. Barker (2012) observes, however, that the Swedish welfare state is a great achievement, but only if you are seen as belonging to it. It has an implicit exclusionary character, and there are tremendous social pressures to conform. The Nordic model has come under increasing pressure with the rise of Right-wing anti-immigration parties (Nardelli and Arnett, 2015) and, as with similar populist parties across Europe, crime and welfare are issues that they seek to exploit.

Narratives of penal policy

As with many other areas of policy, common-sense or widely held views are often spread by images, stories or myths (Taylor, 2003). This seems to be particularly important in the penal field where media representations of crime are so influential. The expansion of the use of imprisonment in both the US and the UK has been driven by a racialised image of young offenders. The meme that Simon (2007) describes as 'governing through crime' – a combination of fear of crime, law and order having a much more powerful impact on the wider political debate and a general public disillusion with alternative to imprisonment – remains very powerful. In the UK context, this has to be combined with a eugenicist discourse focused on the underclass. This has become deeply embedded within the wider popular culture (Slater, 2009, 2012; Jensen, 2013; Tyler, 2013). These developments are important for social work as they largely take place in poor, marginalised communities. Research that examines the underclass discourse is often largely focused on the experiences of women in either poorly paid precarious work or in receipt of welfare.

Prison conditions

Prison conditions must be a key area of concern for social work as a profession if it is to match its stated commitment to human rights. One of the most depressing features of the penal state is the fact that the expansion of the use of imprisonment has been accompanied by deteriorating prison conditions.

The Trenčín Statement (WHO, 2007), which outlines the UN position on the treatment of prisoners, states that 'Prisoners shall have access to the health services available in the country without discrimination on the grounds of their legal situation.'

In England and Wales, HM Inspector of Prisons (HMIP) has overall responsibility for monitoring conditions in the prison estate. The 2013/14 report (HMIP, 2013) gives a very bleak picture of the prison regime. It showed a 69 per cent rise in suicides in prisons in 2013-14, and was described as 'the most unacceptable feature' of a prison system that is experiencing a 'rapid deterioration' in safety standards. The report paints a portrait of prisons where bullying, violence – including sexual violence – and intimidation are commonplace. It also indicates that drugs are widely available while there are often little constructive activities for prisoners in overcrowded institutions.

Conditions including overcrowding, reduced spending on meals and levels of violence and assaults were also highlighted.

The healthcare needs of prisoners reflects the fact that the prison population is overwhelmingly drawn from the most impoverished and marginalised communities. This is true of both mental and physical health. The Royal College of Nursing (RCN) (2004) makes it clear that prisoners have a higher incidence of long-term conditions and chronic disease. These conditions include coronary heart disease, diabetes, mental health issues, substance misuse and HIV. In addition, those groups that are most at risk from these conditions or face the greatest barriers to accessing healthcare are much more likely to be incarcerated. These groups include young men, care leavers, sex workers and IV (intravenous) drug users. The prison environment, including the churn of prisoners and overcrowding, makes the delivery of healthcare problematic. The World Health Organization (WHO) (2013), for example, reports that the rate of tuberculosis is estimated to be 100 times higher in prison than in the general population. Overcrowding, poor nutrition, late diagnosis, poor treatment and transfer of prisoners contribute to its spread.

Since 2000, the rate of imprisonment of women has risen by over 50 per cent (Walmsley, 2013), although women are generally incarcerated at lower rates than men. Following a series of incidents of self-harm and suicides at women's prisons, the Corston Inquiry (2008) was established to examine the treatment of women. On the whole, women are less likely to commit violent or other serious offences than men. One effect of this is that they are generally sentenced to shorter periods in custody – the majority in England and Wales being for six months or less. An impact of the smaller numbers of women in custody is that there are fewer female prisons. Women are thus more likely to be sent to a jail further from their local community, with subsequent impacts on maintaining family links and future reintegration. The Corston Inquiry gives a stark outline of the wider factors in the lives of women in custody: 37 per cent attempted suicide at some time in their life, 51 per cent have severe and enduring mental illness, over 50 per cent had been subjected to domestic abuse, and one in three had been sexually abused. Imprisonment has an impact on the whole family of the incarcerated individual. The Howard League for Penal Reform (2010) describes children as the forgotten victims of mass incarceration. The huge dislocation and disruption created in the lives in the region of 18,000 children whose mothers are imprisoned each year have to be taken into account when calculating any wider benefits of imprisonment. Given the fact that women are, on the whole, involved in non-violent and acquisitive crime, alternatives must be explored.

The rate of incarceration has not reached this level in the UK, but the state continues to use imprisonment at historically astonishing rates. Simon feels that the floodwaters are now receding, revealing the damage that has been done to individuals, communities and wider society. A number of pressures have exposed the internal contradictions of the penal state. In the US, a broader coalition has successfully recast the issues of mass incarceration as issues of civil rights, and this has gained traction. Hillary Clinton, in a 1996 speech in support of the Violent Crime Control Act 1994, the one piece of legislation that is often identified as having a key role in the development of mass incarceration, described young offenders thus:

> They are not just gangs of kids anymore. They are often the kinds of kids that are called "superpredators". No conscience, no empathy. We can talk about why they ended up that way, but first we have to bring them to heel. (C-Span, 1996)

This is a classic example of dog whistle politics as there is no explicit use of racial terms, but the audience will be fully aware that this is appealing to long-standing racist stereotypes.

As part of her campaign for the Democratic nomination, Clinton shifted from this position, recognising that the US justice system needs to be reformed. Alongside these campaigns is recognition that fiscal pressures have led to the questioning of the use of the state's resources in this way. The crash of 2008 has led to retrenchment in public spending, including on imprisonment. It is ironic that one of the consequences of the crash might be a rebalancing of the criminal justice system with an emphasis on community punishment as an alternative to imprisonment. The fact that the motivation for this is fiscal rather than philosophical doesn't make it any less welcome.

Rates of violent crime have been declining. The fear of violent crime and the War on Drugs have been key factors in the development of mass incarceration. As violent crime falls, there is a law of diminishing returns in calls to tackle such crime. However, a note of caution needs to be struck here. These political calls are often aimed at older voters, and this group of voters is less likely to see crime rates as being low. This is not to say that law and order does not remain a very important political and policy issue. It acknowledges that if a society or community feels safer, there is less scope to exploit the issue politically. The War on

Drugs, that is, a harsh punitive response to those involved in any way with using or dealing illegal narcotics, is now widely accepted to be a failure (Gray, 2001; Levy-Pounds, 2010). The Drug Policy Alliance's (2011) analysis of media reporting shows that this failure has been acknowledged around the world. The appeal of harm reduction strategies and a response to substance misuse that is informed by public health principles will have an inevitable impact on reducing prison numbers. And to be sustained, a war requires propaganda and the demonising of an enemy. These processes become much harder to sustain if recreational drug use is more common. In addition, if middle-class children of parents who have used drugs recreationally throughout their adult lives are drawn into the criminal justice system, then wider issues of legitimacy will arise.

Society's response to crime and its system of punishment raises fundamental ethical and philosophical issues. As Beckett and Western (2001) suggest, it is impossible to view penal policy without a broader analysis of social and welfare policies. In their analysis, political cultures that see the roots of offending in social factors such as poverty and marginalisation are much more likely to focus on rehabilitation. This will lead to a greater use of community-based sentences and lower rates of imprisonment. The reverse is also the case. A political culture that sees offending as the result of individual failings will lead to a more punitive approach and higher rates of imprisonment. There is a discernible trend here. Over the past 30 years in the UK there has been a clear shift towards individualism in a whole range of cultural areas. Wilkinson (2000) concludes that a culture such as the US, where competitive individualism is a deeply embedded cultural trope, will see offenders as unreformable. Furthermore, Tonry (1999) argues that more inclusive cultures also provide protection against the sorts of moral panics that occur in response to individual high-profile crimes or offending. For example, Green (2008) explores the contrasting responses in Norway and England to child murders carried out by children. The murder of Jamie Bulger in Liverpool in February 1993 was seen by the media and politicians, including the former Prime Minister, John Major, as symptomatic of a wider and deep-seated moral decline. In stark contrast, the murder of Silje Redergard in Trondheim, Norway, was seen as a tragic one-off, where the perpetrators required expert ongoing intervention with the ultimate aim of their reintegration into society.

In considering questions of punishment and what these processes reveal about any society, it is impossible to avoid the towering figure of Michel Foucault. He often described his work as a 'history of the present'. I take this to be a warning against seeing the period that we are living in as somehow the beginning or the end of a historical process. In the area of punishment, there is a danger of assuming that what we see as brutalities and physical indignities meted out in the name of punishment have been abandoned. The realities of Abu Ghraib or prison regimes closer to home that tolerate or allow violence to flourish should quickly disavow this notion. Foucault's (1977) *Discipline and punish: The birth of the prison* opens with a description of the punishments inflicted on the attempted regicide by Damiens, which are outlined in great detail. To the modern reader, these appear as examples of brutality. Nietzsche, in *On the genealogy of morality* (1998), had concerned himself with the development of social mores. He saw this as a way in which man's elemental impulses were contained. Nietzsche outlines the most gruesome of Old German punishments. These included stoning, boiling in oil or wine and smearing the transgressor with honey and leaving him to bake in the sun. The most prominent feature of these punishments is their physical brutality. Nietzsche and Foucault do not approach such punishments as simple outbursts of savagery. Punishment is a regulated cultural practice. The physical nature of the punishment reflects the belief that crime was considered an offence against the monarch. This is not just the case for Damiens, but for all offenders. The symbols and rituals of punishment reflect the value system of the society that produces it. In this process, Foucault notes that the offender is allowed to denounce the judges before the sentence is carried out. In this way, the established order is overturned for a moment before being restored and reinvigorated by the punishment.

Foucault (1977) contrasts the image of Damiens being pulled apart by horses (having been subjected to a litany of assaults including having molten wax poured on him) with the sombre image of Foucher's prison timetable. For Foucault, this is a paradigmatic shift. The timetable represents the Enlightenment values of rationality. He argues that from the French Revolution onwards, punishment as a public spectacle declined. As the definition of what constituted a crime remained largely unchanged, this shift, Foucault argues, can only be explained by moves in societal values. This does not represent progress, but rather a shift in the ways that social control and domination are exercised. For Foucault, the key feature of the penal or psychiatric system was the struggle of the individual against the wider societal impulses to conform or control. Thus the changes in penal policy he discusses are the beginnings of new technologies of power rather than elements of a humanitarian project to reform brutal regimes. Mass incarceration has as its aim the incapacitation of offenders. One feature of the expansion of the penal state has been overcrowded prisons. This, along with populist moves to make regimes more Spartan, amount to a reversal of the shift outlined by Foucault (1977, 2008). The body of the offender has once again become the site of punishment. Examples of this shift include the recent ban on books being sent to prisoners in England and Wales or the activities of Arizona Sheriff Joe Arpaio. Arpaio prides himself on forcing offenders to wear pink underwear and sleep in tents in the baking local heat, as well as boasting of spending more on food for prison dogs than inmates.

The US has led the way in the expansion of the use of imprisonment, resulting in a huge prison industrial complex that marginalises even further the most disadvantaged urban communities – particularly African-American ones (Garland, 2001; Gottschalk, 2006; Mauer, 2006; Wacquant, 2009b; Drucker, 2011; Alexander, 2012). What Simon (2014) has termed the 'arc of punitiveness' began in the mid-1970s driven by populist response to increases in violent crime and the politicisation of the law and order debate (Simon, 2007). In this regard, the US acts as a clear warning of the potentially huge social, communal and individual damage that the overuse of imprisonment causes. It might be tempting from a European perspective to see these developments as solely the result of the US' history of slavery, Jim Crow and ongoing discrimination. However, there are similar trends in the over-representation of young men from black and minority ethnic (BME) backgrounds. In the UK currently, African-Caribbean citizens are imprisoned at a rate of 6.8 per 1,000 compared to 1.3 per 1,000 among white citizens; 27 per cent of the UK prison population comes from a BME background and over two-thirds of that group are serving sentences of over four years (1990 Trust, 2010). Berman (2012) reports that in June 2011, 13.4 per cent of the prison population, where ethnicity was recorded, was Black or Black British. This group comprises 2.7 per cent of the general population. It was estimated that in 2015, 70 per cent of the French prison population is Muslim the figure in the general population is 8 per cent. It is illegal to collect figures on ethnic background in France, so no official statistics exist. It is also an issue of class, as the overwhelming majority of prisoners come from impoverished backgrounds.

The end of the penal state

Fiscal retrenchment is exposing some of the inherent contradictions within the penal state. In addition, there has been a series of challenges to the operation of penal systems. Social work as a profession can play a role in recasting these issues in terms of human rights. It seems somewhat counter-intuitive to look to the US – the home of the penal state – for a solution to the problems that mass incarceration creates. It should be emphasised that the problems that mass incarceration generates can be solved in isolation from wider social policy considerations. This is one of the key themes of my argument throughout this book. In California, a group of prisoners sued the state, arguing that penal policies amounted to a breach of the 8th Amendment's constitutional prohibition on cruel and unusual punishment. It was argued that prison conditions, including chronic overcrowding and a lack of healthcare, produced an environment where the prisoners' constitutional rights could not be observed. The inevitable result of imprisoning more people for longer was the collapse of a prison healthcare system. Justice Kennedy, who wrote the majority decision in *Brown vs Plata*, was so appalled by the conditions that existed that he included photographs in the Supreme Court Judgment, the first time that this had happened. The photographs represent the human impact of the penal crisis in California, and include scenes of chronic overcrowding and 'dry cells' – essentially cages used as holding cells for people waiting for transfer to mental health facilities.

Judge Kennedy concluded that:

> … prisoners retain the essence of human dignity…. A prison that deprives prisoners of basic sustenance, including adequate medical care, is incompatible with the concept of human dignity and has no place in a civilized society. (Brown v. Plata, 134 S. Ct. 1 [U.S. 2013])

The notion of dignity can form the basis for a recalibration of social, welfare and penal policies. The final chapter addresses these issues in more depth.

The Strangeways Riot in 1990, a previous moment of crisis for the British penal system, occurred at a time when the prison population was roughly half of what it is in 2017. The riot was the biggest in UK penal history. Lord Woolf chaired the Inquiry into the riot, and the report that was subsequently published in 1991 identified overcrowding and poor conditions as the root causes of the disturbances. 'Slopping out' – where prisoners use a bucket as a toilet and empty it out each morning – was still common practice at this time, and was not abolished in England until 1995. The report provided a blueprint for reform of the prison system, including a shift away from the use of imprisonment for all but the most serious offences. The Home Office developed policies to reduce imprisonment on the basis that 'prison is an expensive way of making bad people worse.' These liberal moves were abandoned under subsequent governments committed to the idea that 'prison works' (Gottschalk, 2006).

The key criticisms of the Woolf (1991) report continue to have resonance. It is perhaps an indication of the crisis point that prisons have reached that Woolf has written the Foreword to a recent report, *A presumption against imprisonment* (Allen et al, 2014). It calls for a radical rethink on penal policy. The key argument is that as a society, we need to reduce the use of imprisonment – it should not be the default sentence. A much clearer framework needs to be developed. To achieve this, the report recommends using diversion from the courts more extensively – promoting greater use of alternative forms of sentences; prohibiting or restricting the imposition of short custodial sentences; removing or restricting the sanction of imprisonment for certain offences; reviewing sentence lengths; and removing mentally disordered and addicted people from prisons (Allen et al, 2014). Such policies chime with core social work values, and are based on an implicit recognition of the inherent dignity of individuals.

The four countries of the UK have very different legal systems, including in their approach to offending. In the Scottish system, social work has maintained a key role in penal policy. I would suggest that it therefore offers a model for an approach that could re-establish social work in England. Scotland's 21st Century Social Work Review Group proposes that 'Reducing re-offending is essentially concerned with the achievement of positive change in the lives of offenders' (McNeill et al, 2005). This statement is based on a welfare approach that recognises that reducing offending, which is the only way to increase public protection, has to be based on an approach that promotes the social inclusion of offenders. The promotion of social inclusion is one of the key tasks and skills of social workers. Social workers can achieve this by building positive relationships with offenders. This is essentially a call for a strengthening of the social work approach and an end to managerialism and bureaucratic practice. It would be naive, however, to assume that such a change will occur overnight. Punitive approaches remain popular and deeply entrenched in public discourse. One of the roles for social work as a profession is to challenge effectively what Wacquant (2009a) terms the 'doxa' of neoliberal penality, manifest in empty slogans such as 'zero tolerance' and 'prison works'. It can do this from a position of moral and empirical strength.

This analysis of current trends in penal policy and the potential that they create for a re-engagement of social work with the criminal justice system is influenced by Stuart Hall's use of the term derived from Marx and Gramsci, of 'conjuncture'. Conjuncture is simply a combination of events. However, Hall uses it as a tool for analysis of the current political and cultural trends. Hall was seeking to move away from the rigid economic determinism of Marxism, arguing that it is important to consider cultural developments. An economic analysis, Hall suggests, only takes one so far (Cummins, 2014). Thus the economic will impact on penal policy in that it will be seen as too expensive, but the cultural can also play a role. If social attitudes to the use of drugs change, as they have, it becomes more difficult to create a 'War on Drugs'. A shift that sees drug use as essentially a health issue will lead to a more social welfare-based response. This creates possibilities for social workers alongside health and social care professions more generally. Throughout the past 30 years, individual workers within the criminal justice system have carved out creative spaces where they can continue to practice in a way that has more in common with notions of rehabilitation than risk management. These processes are very much in their early stages, and such developments are not linear. Of course, it is possible that this analysis is over-optimistic or that any progress will be derailed by a moral panic around a high-profile crime or crimes. However, there is a role for individual social workers, academics and the wider profession to influence penal policy. The criminal justice system should be a key area of concern for the profession and the academy. Social work needs to forcefully make the case that imprisonment fails on its own terms, and has a devastating impact on individuals, families and communities. Rediscovering notions of dignity and developing policies based on it are the place to start. Scottish policy in this field provides some clear directions for future policy development.

Conclusion

This chapter has examined the development of welfare and penal policies over the past 35 years. Bourdieu's conception of the state argues that it has two poles – the *left hand* and the *right hand*. The left represents the welfare and social provision of state services – health, education and other forms of community investment. The right represents the police, Courts and the penal system. There are some difficulties with accepting such a binary division between these elements of the state, however. It has always been the case that there is an overlap between these functions – the benefits system is also a disciplinary one, for example. Roberts (1999) demonstrates the way that the US system has been used as a way of limiting the reproductive rights of poor black women, for example. The examples outlined above of 'sanctions' that have been imposed or the WCA scheme show that the balance can and does shift. It is also clear that certain areas of the welfare system are seen as more benign or perhaps less disciplinary in function than others. It should also be acknowledged that institutions of the right hand of the state have the potential to act within what might be termed a welfare role. Policing is a good example of this, as it is not simply about its core function of maintaining order or detecting and apprehending offenders. Police officers searching for a missing person are, I would argue, acting in a welfare role. There are always tensions in these areas, both for organisations involved in turf wars, and also for individual practitioners. Social work as a profession continues to struggle with these debates. On the one hand, it has a commitment to social justice; on the other, it is often experienced as being disciplinary or overly bureaucratic.

In this chapter, I have argued that the welfare and penal systems cannot be looked at in isolation; they are inextricably linked. In addition, they cannot be examined in isolation from wider society. Martinson's (1974) statement that in penal policy 'nothing works' shows that there has been a shift in emphasis to identifying and subsequent attempts to manage risk. Penal policy has reflected or even led wider changes in society, with a fundamental shift from the 'disciplinary gaze'. Offenders are no longer seen as individuals who need to be rehabilitated so that they can become fully functioning members of society. They are, rather, seen as a threat that needs to be managed – the living embodiment of Beck's (1992) 'risk society'.

Bauman argues (2008) that we have seen the development of what he terms the 'personal security state'. One of the key ways in which the modern state claims legitimacy is by its ability to defend its subjects. In modern society, these threats or perceived threats are increasingly internal or domestic ones. Wacquant has argued that the US welfare state has been dismantled while incarceration rates have grown exponentially, that welfare has been replaced by prisonfare. The US welfare state that did not offer European levels of protection has been swept away. In its place, mass incarceration has taken on the role of the management of the urban, largely black and male urban poor. As welfare has contracted in the US, the UK and other liberal democracies, the penal state in all its forms has expanded.

Since the economic crisis of the 1970s, political legitimacy has been increasingly maintained through the prism or metaphor of penal policy. Brady (2009) demonstrates that despite high economic growth in both the UK and US in the 1990s and 2000s, rates of poverty have increased in both countries. In contrast, countries with stronger welfare tradition and provision, for example, Sweden, have not experienced such increases. The retrenchment of welfare provision clearly impacts disproportionately on the poor, and these trends have been exacerbated by austerity.

FIVE

Poverty, inequality and contemporary social work

Context of contemporary social work practice

This chapter begins with a consideration of the broader current position of social work. It is important to begin with a clear statement outlining the fundamentals of the approach adopted here. Poverty and inequality are fundamental issues of social justice and human rights. As such, they are legitimate and appropriate areas for social work concern. My analysis is informed by Fraser (1995), who identifies two distinct but interrelated forms of stratification in modern societies. The first is the unequal distribution of economic resources. The second Webb (2010, p 2365) outlines thus: a 'cultural order of recognition relations – relating to gender, ethnicity, age and sexuality – that generate inequalities of status.' Within this cultural order, the status of being poor or living in poverty has increasingly taken on the form of a cultural identity. As Chapter 3 illustrates, it is a marginalised status that has had a whole series of stereotypical views ascribed to it. Following Fraser (1995), I argue that these orders of stratification and recognition are distinct, but they are also inseparable:

> Even the most material economic institutions have a constitutive, irreducible cultural dimension; they are shot through with significations and norms. Conversely, even the most discursive cultural practices have a constitutive, irreducible political economic dimension; they are underpinned by material supports. (Fraser, 1995, p 720)

It is impossible to separate the development of policies such as austerity that target the poor and marginalised without examining how those groups are consistently represented within the discourses of popular culture. As argued in previous chapters, shame and experiences of humiliation are consistent features of the daily lives of those who are marginalised from mainstream society. These may take physical and other forms, as reported by Crisis (Sanders and Albanese, 2016, p 2):

- More than one in three have been deliberately hit, kicked, or experienced some other form of violence while homeless.
- Over one in three (34%) have had things thrown at them.
- Almost one in 10 (9%) have been urinated on while homeless. More than one in 20 (7%) have been the victim of a sexual assault.
- Almost half (48%) have been intimidated or threatened with violence whilst homeless.
- Six in 10 (59%) have been verbally abused or harassed.

The preceding chapters of this book have argued that neoliberalism followed the set of economy policies called 'austerity', and an attempt at full realisation of the neoliberal political project has created a more unequal society. Not only has society become more unequal, but also, at the same time, there has been a demonisation of the 'poor' – not poverty, but the poor. These processes are clearly two sides of the same coin. Part of the process of undermining the foundations of the welfare state is to present it as dependency-producing and over-generous. Within this strategy of anti-welfarism, certain groups, for example, asylum-seekers and refugees, are targeted as part of a never explicitly acknowledged but highly racialised discourse. This is a recasting of the tropes of an attack on black and Irish immigrants from the 1950s onwards. Alongside these racial elements, anti-welfarism features a large dose of classism and misogyny. As noted in the discussion of the media portrayals of Mick Philpott and Karen Matthews in Chapter 3, these totally unrepresentative cases of violent crime are used to stand for the whole of the welfare system. Alongside these huge economic, social and cultural changes, social work as a profession has undergone significant developments. Like all areas of public services, it has seen a growth in the audit and inquiry culture, which has developed alongside a cult of managerialism. The overall result is that social work is being expected to do more with less. Alongside these increasing demands, managerialism involves a challenge to traditional social work approaches and values.

This is a very gloomy description of the current position – social workers face huge challenges, and feel that their professional autonomy has been consistently undermined. Fenton (2014) argues that social workers of the current generation are much less critical of the surge of managerialism. Obviously, the day-to-day demands of practice may mean that social workers focus on getting the job done. Bauman (2000) notes that there is a danger that the ethical demands of social work as a profession can be marginalised. He suggests that, in what he calls a period of 'liquid modernity', dependence or relationships that cannot be monetised are deemed inferior. Those who can take part in globalised markets are failed consumers. Social work has to be rooted in the ethical impulse that generates a respect and concern for others. Bauman's *Modernity and the Holocaust* (1989) is a study of the bureaucracy that underpinned and enabled the Holocaust. Arendt (1963) cautions against the danger of creating systems where individuals follow rather than question rules. Bauman (2000) argues that the more the 'essential human and moral aspects of care' are hidden by rules, regulations and procedures, the more distant it becomes from its original ethical purpose. The ethics of good social work practice cannot be separated from its organisation.

The danger of managerialism is that it creates an environment where social workers are too exhausted or frightened to ask critical questions of organisations where they work or of policy-makers. The result is that good people can unthinkingly or even with the best of motives do wrong or harmful things. And language has a key role to play here. All professions use jargon or shorthand that they should not. However, social work practice has become dominated by a series of phrases – *LAC*, *disguised compliance*, *disorganised attachment* and *toxic trio* – these have, to my mind, come to represent a bureaucratic approach that has lost sense of the fact that social workers work with people. People have complex identities, so to use an abbreviation like 'LAC' is simply unprofessional and uncaring in my view. I cannot conceive of circumstances where professionals would not know the name of the child and it could not be used. If writing a report about the experiences of 'looked-after children', then the full term should be used. The important thing here is that power and language are connected. This is part of a process – perhaps unintentional – of 'Othering', creating an identity. 'LAC', for example, is imbued with a series of notions that wider society has about children who are in public care.

Disguised compliance is an example of a phrase that has become almost diagnostic. Hart (2017) traces the origins and use of the term. It is meant to capture the fact that some families appear to cooperate with social services but do not actually comply with child protection plans. I use it here as an example of a term that has come, for me, to symbolise a bureaucratised practice that has potentially lost touch with Bauman's notion of an ethical impulse. Hart points out that the term, despite its ubiquity, is actually meaningless. It would be hard, if not impossible, to disguise compliance. Despite this, as Hart notes, the NSPCC posted the following on its website:

Disguised compliance involves parents giving the appearance of cooperating with child welfare agencies to avoid raising suspicions and allay concerns. Published case reviews highlight that professionals sometimes delay or avoid interventions due to parental disguised compliance. (NSPCC website, quoted by Hart, 2017)

NSPCC training materials identify five possible signs of potential disguised non-compliance: (1) deflecting attention, (2) criticising professionals, (3) tidying the house before arranged visits, (4) promising to take up services then not doing so, and (5) avoiding contact with professionals.

Hart unpicks these with the skill of a barrister. Number (5) is completely meaningless, as avoiding contact does not clearly involve any attempt at disguise. Number (1), where it is alleged that parents engage with one set of professionals to deflect attention, requires a level of planning that is not readily apparent. Families in these circumstances are more likely to have similar attitudes to all professionals involved. Hart concludes that the attraction of the phrase is that it has a pseudo-scientific air. It also becomes a 'diagnosis' – it appears to be offering an explanation whereas, in reality, it is a poor substitute for proper assessment and evidence. Furthermore, it is based, to my mind, on a fundamental suspicion of all parents' motives. It places them in a position where they cannot win – if they tidy up before social workers visit, it is suspicious, and if they do not, they are part of a 'feckless underclass'.

The underclass discourse is ultimately a pathologising, dehumanising and depersonalising one. There is a danger that the response and challenge to it produces an equally distorted narrative that sees individuals in difficult economic and social circumstances as passive victims. Lister's (2004a) work can be used as a starting point for social workers to avoid this and idealised or romantic notions of rescue. Ziv (cited in Saar-Heiman et al, 2017) has described poverty as an 'insidious trauma', which is the result of a damaging ongoing social reality. This acknowledged the potential psychosocial and material damage that poverty can create. Gupta et al (2014) show that children living in poverty face an increased range of adverse social outcomes in terms of health, education, and so on. Younge (2017), in his discussion of knife crime in London, makes an explicit link between cuts in social provision for young people and increases in the rate of crime. The important point here is that there is an incremental impact of cuts in social provision. While accepting these points, it is important not to fall into the trap of presenting people in poverty as spectators who need to be the targets of support. Ranciere (2004) emphasised that the poor are a category of people whose views are seen as worthless or beneath consideration. There are complex issues here as the advocacy role of social work involves raising these issues in the public sphere. While doing so, social work needs to avoid a top-down model or the lecturing or hectoring tones that have marked previous approaches.

Lister produced a taxonomy of the potential ways in which individuals and families respond to living in poverty. This emphasises agency, and also the fact that there are a range of experiences. People respond to the adversity that living in poverty produces in complex and subtle ways.

Lister (2004a) argues that debates about poverty are being increasingly recast in 'a non-materialist discourse of human and citizenship rights, democracy, inclusion and respect.' This is, of course, not to deny the material reality of the day-to-day lives of people who are struggling. However, this shift in focus does enable debates to shift from continuous technical debates about the measurement of poverty. The statistical measurement of poverty and inequality is, of course, very important – debates about poverty cannot take place in some sort of statistical vacuum. However, we also need to emphasise that poverty is a daily experience for people. One of the main themes of the arguments presented here is that social work and social workers need to focus on this social justice perspective. Lister (2015) emphasises that agency has to be placed within the context of the broader structural constraints that impact on lives. Class inequalities and the issues of race, gender and disability are factors that need to be taken into account here. There is a dividing line between acknowledging agency (which, of course, means recognising that individuals make mistakes) and blaming people for poverty. Wealthier people, like all of us, make mistakes; they simply have more resources to fall back on.

Lister's taxonomy

Lister's taxonomy (2004b) is based on two axes – everyday to strategic and the personal to the political/citizen. In the four quadrants 'getting by', 'getting (back) at', 'getting out' and 'getting organised' appear. This taxonomy of agency can also be used as the basis for the positioning of anti-poverty social work. Lister states that 'getting by' should not be underestimated, as a whole body of research indicates that skill and hard work is required. The notion of 'getting by' also incorporates precarity and insecurity. Poverty and lack of resources mean that it is much more difficult to deal with sudden unexpected expenditure. Limited disposable income obviously makes it much more difficult to save. It is clear that the use of food banks has been driven, in part, by these sorts of circumstances. The shock is regrettably one that is a state-imposed benefit sanctions. Insecurity is at the heart of the experience of poverty. Lister notes that responsibility for managing or negotiating this still lies mainly with women. Tirado (2014), in her blog, which became her book *Hand to mouth*, captures both these experiences.

Lister suggests that 'getting (back) at' includes undeclared paid work, as this is a way of resisting the system. There are some potential difficulties with this argument, however, not least that it is ultimately self-defeating. However, it does highlight the fact that in other areas of work life, 'getting one over' the system is usually celebrated – certainly in the popular cultural portrayal of the ducking and diving wheeler-dealer. Tirado and others' work is a more discursive form of resistance.

'Getting out' is the quadrant of Lister's model where agency and structure are to be analysed. Poverty is often presented as a life or even intergenerational sentence. There are clearly examples of individuals who grow up in poverty but who subsequently enjoy more secure or even wealthy lifestyles. There is a danger of using these examples to obscure the barriers or the odds that individuals have to overcome. The work of Shildrick and MacDonald (2013) is important here in demonstrating that the current structure of the labour market makes it difficult for even the most motivated to escape the low pay/no pay cycle. The structural barriers that this research highlights include access to childcare, public transport or lack of a car and the nature of jobs available – short-term or minimum wage work.

The final quadrant, 'getting organised', refers to collective action. It would be falling into the trap of regarding the poor as passive to ignore the wave of community and other work that exists. However, on the broad political scale, Lister notes that there are a series of philosophical and organisational barriers here that serve to reduce the potential for collective action. One significant barrier is the fact that 'poor' does not or may not constitute a part of any individual's identity. There are numerous community groups campaigning on issues of poverty but that do not necessarily identify explicitly as such. Food banks might possibly to be seen in this way. Trade union movements have traditionally played a key role in the political organisation of the working class. One of the undoubted 'successes' (on its own terms) of neoliberalism has been the weakening of the trade union movement, as the structure of the labour market makes it even more difficult for unions to recruit and retain new members.

Social work approaches

Viewing issues of poverty and inequality as key questions with which social workers need to grapple is not an argument for greater intervention. For example, the work of Bywaters and others discussed below, which examines the links between poverty and children and families' social work, is not, as I read it, a call for more intervention in the lives of individual poor families. It is, I would argue, a call for greater social investment. It is highlighting the dangers of poverty being recast as a form of parental neglect. Parents living in poverty should not automatically be viewed as lacking parental capacity – they merely lack resources. The view that poverty is, somehow, an indicator of parental inadequacy is one that, as we have seen, has very long historical roots (Welshman, 2013). It has, however, been given a recent boost by the seemingly inexorable rise of Dame Louise Casey and the Troubled Families Agenda (Casey, 2016). Social work in this, as in other fields, needs to find a way to support families and communities without pathologising whole groups in the community. This becomes increasingly difficult in a period where policies, particularly in the area of children and families' social work, are increasingly premised on a notion of early intervention, early intervention here being a euphemism for greater state involvement and intervention in the lives of poorer families.

Webb (2010) notes that the redistribution/recognition dilemma is not a simply theoretical debate. It is one that is real and not simply resolvable. Fraser (1997) argues that we must seek approaches that minimise the dilemma where both must be pursued. As well as arguing for and supporting policies that tackle injustice and inequality, social work as a profession and individual workers can challenge the cultural practices that lead to misrecognition. This can take many forms, whether it be supporting campaigns for the rights of asylum-seekers and refugees or challenging the myths of poverty porn. In the next chapter I discuss the possibility of using the works of Emmanuel Levinas as a basis for an approach that avoids 'Othering', but start from a position of the need to recognise a duty to fellow humans on the basis of their humanity alone, rather than any other qualities or characteristics they may have.

One of Lipsky's (1980) key insights into the functioning of modern welfare and public service systems is that the front line workers are not only representative of the organisation, they also often have to subvert or resist policies to either make them work or meet the needs of the groups with whom they work. Bourdieu et al (1999, p 184) see these processes as a form of collective 'double consciousness' that expose or are 'shot through with the contradictions of the State.'The liminal position of social work and social workers is one of its most complex, but also, to my mind, one of its most interesting features. Bourdieu (2005) notes that such a role generates a number of struggles or contradictions for those who see themselves as progressives but work for a state or government that does not share or is often opposed to these views. Social work, particularly in the areas of child protection, work with asylum-seekers and refugees and mental health services, is an example of this dilemma.

Backwith (2015) notes that while many social workers are committed to tackling poverty, it is still curiously absent from many discussions of the role of the profession. It is the one feature of many service users and their families' lives that is consistently overlooked or marginalised. There is a need for social work and social workers to consider why this might be the case. As discussed earlier, social work is not a monolith – some social workers may well agree with the approach that sees poverty as the result of individuals' failings or poor choices. This is an argument that has always existed in modern social work. It can be seen in the contrasting approaches of, for example, the Charity Organisation Society (CSO) and the Settlement Movement. The CSO focused very much on work with the 'deserving poor'. Their work can be viewed as a form of 'missionary work' with the urban poor bringing middle-class values. The Settlement Movement – its most famous participant being Clement Attlee – would be seen much more as a community-based and educative approach.

Social work has struggled to shake off the legacy of the CSO approach. The 'Lady Bountiful' stereotype of the middle-class person doing what they deem to be 'good works' may have morphed into or been replaced by the sandals and sock-wearing PC radical stereotype. What both unfair portrayals of social work have in common is a disconnect between social workers and service users. Social work sees itself as concerned with fundamental issues of dignity, citizenship and the empowerment of marginalised groups. However, far too often, despite the best efforts of individual social workers, this is not how those using social services experience social work processes. Strier and Binyamin (2013) show that social work is often experienced as bureaucratic and dehumanising. Jargon and the use of a rhetoric that does not reflect the daily reality of individual lives do not assist here. The bureaucratised and over-management of current social work practice is clearly a factor. All professions will have some jargon. Social work, ironically, given its claims of being focused on individuals, families and communities, is a serial offender in this regard.

One of the fundamental dilemmas that individual social workers face is how to practice in a way that acknowledges and tackles poverty. This becomes more difficult if agency and organisational structures focus on risk assessment and other approaches that restrict individual staff autonomy and creativity. (The final chapter discusses some of these issues in more depth.) If we see poverty as an issue of human rights, then anti-poverty practice is part of wider anti-oppressive practice. Parrot (2014) suggests that to practice in an effectively anti-oppressive manner, social work has to be systematic. He outlines a four-part process:

- Assess: explore service users's needs using a strengths based approach
- Plan: reach an agreement as to how those needs are to be met
- Intervene: carry out the agreed plan into action
- Evaluate: review and evaluate the plan

This has a surface appeal, and it certainly offers students and new practitioners a model for beginning in practice. It has echoes of a task-centred approach and the same attractions of a structure. The difficulty with this, as with similar essentially models of planning for casework, is that they do not examine in sufficient depth the wider social and political context of social work practice. Social work resources are under increasing pressure, and one of the dangers of superficially appealing phrases such as 'strengths perspectives' is that they can be used as a mask for the rationing of services. If your strengths are such that you are not deemed to need a service but you feel that you need one, I am not clear what the next steps should be – working with the service user so that they realise that they have more strengths than they realise?

Bronfenbrenner (1979) argued that traditional approaches to developmental psychology had overlooked or marginalised the environmental and social factors that have an impact on the development of a child. In his schema, development is shaped by the interaction between the individual and the environment in which they are brought up. Environmental factors include individuals and institutions – families, parents and schools, for example – but also broader historical and cultural forces. Taking this ecological approach would force us to see poverty as an important factor, and also to view the issue in structural terms. Bronfenbrenner's work was influential in helping to establish the Head Start programme in the US, a programme that provides early childhood education and related advice on health and nutrition. This was a model for the Sure Start scheme that New Labour then introduced. Bronfenbrenner's influence can also be seen in the Common Assessment Framework (CAF) as 'family and environmental factors' form the base of the triangle of the assessment. However, social work practice and intervention have tended to focus on one of the sides of the triangle, 'parenting capacity'.

Bradshaw (2011) identifies the impacts of poverty as: higher mortality and morbidity, lack of resources and opportunities, mental ill health, poor housing and poor neighbourhoods. It is interesting that the stigma attached to poverty or living in a poor neighbourhood is not as prominent here. In addition to this list we need to consider the impact that poverty has on the parents and carers of children. It is increasingly recognised that poverty is much more diffuse, in the sense that there are pockets of deprivation in areas that are generally thought of as wealthy. For example, Manchester is generally viewed as a dynamic city with a thriving economy – particularly in the areas of media and law – with a world-famous university, two high-profile football clubs and great nightlife (so my younger colleagues and students inform me). However, in 2014, Ofsted's inspection of children's services in the city revealed that:

- 36.6% of the local authority's children are living in poverty
- The proportion of children entitled to free school meals in primary schools is 35.4% (the national average is 18.1%)
- The proportion of children entitled to free school meals in secondary schools is 33.8% (the national average is 15.1%)

The report itself judged overall that services for children in the city were inadequate. It makes no mention of the extent of poverty or its potential impact. The bare facts are that over a third of children in the city are living in poverty. These children are obviously living across the city, so there are areas where the extent of poverty is much higher than this – a shocking figure of over a third.

I use the areas of children and families' social work, mental health practice and work with asylum-seekers and refugees as a means of exploring the complex relationship between poverty, social work and social justice. Poverty and the conditions of living in poverty have always been means of controlling the poor and marginalised (Cohen, 2006). As we have seen throughout the past 15 years, the UK has become a more unequal society. One of the features of these developments that is often overlooked is that they are most keenly experienced by children.

We saw in Chapter 2 that there has been a shift that has seen younger people more likely to experience poverty than older and retired people, although child poverty fell under the Labour government in the period to 2010 (Toynbee and Walker, 2011).

There are a number of complexities and contradictions that needed to be explored when we consider the links between poverty and intervention by the state. Donzelot (1979) noted that poorer families have consistently been subject to greater state surveillance than wealthier ones. The increase in state surveillance will almost inevitably lead to greater intervention. This is a combination of increased contact and also the influence of a series of stigmatising assumptions about poorer families. As many commentators point out, deprivation itself does not provide a complete or an adequate account of why some parents are regarded as being unable to meet the basic care needs of their children. Work in the field of resilience shows that a complex range of factors need to be examined to understand how some families, groups and communities manage and respond to crisis (Orthner et al, 2004; Sanchez-Jankowski, 2008; Distelberg and Taylor, 2013; McArthur and Winkworth, 2016).

It is a dangerous fallacy to equate living in poverty with parental neglect – one that as we shall see is increasingly being made. Tobis (2013) and Featherstone et al (2014) show the ways that child protection systems in New York and England and Wales can become punitive and lose core humanistic values. As Featherstone et al (2014) suggest, the result is that parents (usually mothers) living in poverty are portrayed as the cause of the difficulties they and their children face. Such an individualised approach leads to a very individualised response. Hayes and Spratt (2014) see an increasing forensic or investigatory turn in child protection. The danger is that a model of practice develops where intervention occurs – no support being offered – at a time of acute crisis, and is of the most dramatic kind, that is, the removal of children from parents. This was certainly how Child Welfare Services in New York functioned before the establishment of the project described by Tobis (2013). In the work that Tobis outlines, parents often felt that there was 'no way back'. This phrase summed up the feeling that even if they did tackle the personal issues – often drug and alcohol issues they faced – they were still huge barriers for them to overcome if they were to be reunited with their children.

This is the context in which the work of Bywaters (2015a) and Bywaters et al (2014a) must be considered. Bywaters et al (2014a) note that the neglect and emotional abuse that is officially recognised or investigated occurs within the context of poverty. To put it another way, those children who state are most likely to see at risk of neglect and abuse are poor. As the authors show, these responses produce or assist in the development of a culture that is a shaming one for parents. It fails to examine the wider factors involved. It also contributes to the often hostile parent–services relationship that Tobis (2013) and Featherstone et al (2104) have outlined. Thorpe et al (2012) show that parents often reject any offers of voluntary support.

Earlier chapters of this book outlined the impacts of neoliberalism and the shifts in social policy that have accompanied it. With a brief hiatus under the first New Labour administration, the general direction of travel has been in a punitive direction (Wacquant, 2009a, 2009b; Tyler, 2013). In addition, there has also been an increase in inequalities. These societal changes require a shift in the approach to child welfare issues and the role of the state including statutory social work services (Featherstone et al, 2014). Child welfare has increasingly become a site for the reproduction and reinforcement of inequalities. The poor social outcomes that children who have been in public care experience has led to debates about the nature of intervention. Forrester et al (2009), in an attempt to move the debate away from a simplistic 'care fails children', argued that this approach did not take account of the damaging experiences that brought children into care. This is an argument for greater earlier intervention. Such moves would clearly represent a huge shift in the balance between individuals, families and the state – a restriction of Howe's (2014) social space. The current moves in the area of adoption reflect these underlying political and cultural shifts.

Munro (2010) outlines the complex nature of the links between social deprivation, concerns about parental capacity and ultimately, statutory intervention. Munro is calling here for greater acknowledgement of the complexity of social work practice and the nature of the risks involved. This is accompanied by a call for an organisational culture that gives great respect to professional autonomy. This would inevitably involve public acknowledgement of the fact that it is simply impossible for social workers or wider society to ensure that all children will be safe at all times. This is obviously not a council of despair, saying that there is nothing that can be done. It is, rather, recognition of the limits of the powers of public services. Warner (2015) demonstrates that the emotional climate in which child protection and welfare policies and developed make this an unpalatable statement – certainly one that no politician could or would make.

There is increasing research examining the intersection between deprivation and the role of child protection services (Bywaters,

2015a; Bilson and Martin, 2016). Using data from the Department for Education, Bywaters shows that a child living in Blackpool, one of the most deprived towns in England, was eight times more likely to be in the care of the local authority than a child in Richmond. Another way of looking at the differential rates of state intervention is to examine the use of child protection plans (CPPs). In 2012, the local authority with the lowest rate of CPPs was Milton Keynes, with a rate of 8.9 per 10,000, compared with the highest rate in Torbay, of 114.8 per 10,000. To put this another way, services in Torbay intervened in this fashion in nearly 13 times as many children's lives as their colleagues in Milton Keynes. One would expect there to be differences, but such huge variations require closer scrutiny.

Bilson and Martin's (2016) analysis of referrals to children's services examines data from 75 per cent of all children's services departments in England which have responsibility for the oversight of the welfare of over half a million children. The aftermath of the case of 'Baby P' has led to an increase in child protection investigations. Bilson and Martin (2016) show that there has been a 79.4 per cent increase in the number of investigations in the five years 2009/10 to 2014/15 – up from 89,300 to 160,200. The number of cases where there was an investigation but the conclusion was that children had not been maltreated had more than doubled from 45,000 to 98,000. As Bilson and Martin note, more children were investigated without finding evidence of maltreatment than the total number of investigations in 2009/10.

The impact of the 'politics of outrage' following the 'Baby P' case would account for some of the increase (Parton, 2012, 2014; Warner, 2013), but these figures remain astonishing. The impact on the nature of the relationship between social workers and the communities that they serve has to be considered here. In this research, data indicated that fewer than 40 per cent of investigations led to a CPP. Any investigation that fundamentally questions a parent or carer's capacity to look after a child is bound to be a stressful process for all involved – children, parents, the wider family and the social workers. Bilson and Martin (2016) argue that the increasing rejection and lack of voluntary support means that pressures on families increase – via investigations – but there is a reduced likelihood that children will receive support. Department for Education (2015) figures show that for the period 2009/10 to 2014/15 there has been a 28 per cent rise in the number of CPPs because of neglect, and a 7.9 per cent increase in the number of children in care. The number of children adopted or placed in special guardianship increased by 93.4 per cent in this period.

Figure 5.1 sums up the impact of these developments.

Figure 5.1: Referrals and investigations in an 'average' class of 30 five-year-olds

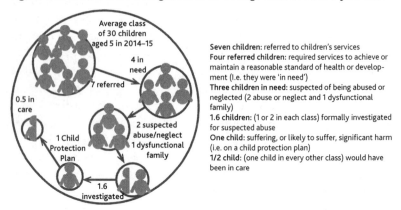

Seven children: referred to children's services
Four referred children: required services to achieve or maintain a reasonable standard of health or development (I.e. they were 'in need')
Three children in need: suspected of being abused or neglected (2 abuse or neglect and 1 dysfunctional family)
1.6 children: (1 or 2 in each class) formally investigated for suspected abuse
One child: suffering, or likely to suffer, significant harm (i.e. on a child protection plan)
1/2 child: (one child in every other class) would have been in care

Note: This figure illustrates the proportions of children reaching different stages of the child protection system if the results of the Freedom of Information request were seen in an 'average' class of 30 children.

Source: Bilson and Martin (2016)

It is worth restating that poverty is not, in and of itself, an explanation for child abuse and neglect. However, as Bywaters et al (2014a) note, the overwhelming majority of what the state recognises as neglect and abuse takes place within environments where children and their families are living in poverty. Pelton (2015) sees a direct link between structural inequalities and the pressures that they produce and potential parenting outcomes. A slightly different approach sees the impact of poverty as creating stress that results in issues such as alcohol and substance misuse that, in turn, impact on parenting (Bywaters, 2015a). Both these perspectives share a fundamental concern with the impact of societal inequalities and poverty. As demonstrated, the alternative view that either denies poverty as a causal factor (Narey, 2014) or argues that social work practice cannot tackle these broader social issues also has to concentrate on the here-and-now of working with children at risk (Kohl et al, 2009). Garrett (2002) argued, at the height of New Labour, that poverty had been airbrushed from the main discourse of the social work profession. One of the key themes in this book is that this process has continued apace since that time, and has been accompanied by an individualistic moralising discourse that Narey's approach so clearly encapsulates. Social work needs to challenge this – even more so when it comes from within the profession. I should make it clear that I am not talking about Narey's review here. Social work, while working with individual families, has to champion ecological approaches and the building of social capital to challenge inequalities. In this context, I am thinking of approaches such as the FAST Model (McDonald et al, 2015) which focus on whole community engagement. Rather than identifying individual families, FAST works with parents and families in vulnerable communities focusing on developing links with schools. I struggle to see how any complete, professional assessment can be of any value if it ignores the material and financial conditions in which a child and family are living.

Mental health

There is not the space here to go over the debates about the social and medical models of mental illness. A pure medical model that sees mental illness as purely the result of brain chemistry and ignores the impact of social factors seems to be completely out-dated (Campbell and Davidson, 2012). Few, if any, mental health professionals would seek to explain mental distress solely in terms of brain chemistry. In a frank and illuminating discussion of his research career, the eminent psychiatrist, Sir Robin Murray stated, 'In the last two decades, it has become obvious that child abuse, urbanization, migration, and adverse life events contribute to the aetiology of schizophrenia and other psychoses' (Murray, 2016, p 254).

Mental health professionals now not only seek to explain mental distress using a variant of a biopsychosocial model; they also recognise that people who experience mental distress continue to face stigma. Cummins' (2011, 2015) analysis of the media reporting of the case of Christopher Clunis shows that stereotypes, often supported by a racialised discourse and imagery, continue to dominate representations of mental illness. Mental illness is often explicitly linked to violent crime in a media-generated risk narrative. The failings of community care were the result of a combination of an idealised rhetoric of community and the fact that the policy was introduced during a period of neoliberal-inspired financial retrenchment. The ambitious aims and civic ideals of the challenge to the indignities of the asylum (Barton, 1959; Goffman, 1963; Martin, 1985) were never fully realised (Knowles, 2000). The previous dominant image of the wild madman chained in an asylum was replaced by that of a homeless, acutely mentally ill man, pushing all his belongings in a shopping cart around the centre of major cities (Cross, 2010). Kelly (2005) has adopted the term 'structural violence' from Liberation Theology as a means of exploring the impact of race, poverty, homelessness and mental illness. Within the broad field of mental health, there are still persistent, seemingly deeply entrenched, issues of discrimination. Omonira-Oyekanmi (2014a) emphasises that it is still the case that young black men are still more likely to be detained under the Mental Health Act, restrained, or to be highly medicated.

In 2004, the Office of the Deputy Prime Minister (OPDM) published a report, *Mental health and social exclusion*. Its main conclusions were as follows:

> 1. Adults with long-term mental health problems are one of the most excluded groups in society. Although many want to work, fewer than a quarter actually do – the lowest employment rate for any of the main groups of disabled people.
>
> 2. Mental health problems are estimated to cost the country over £77 billion a year through the costs of care, economic losses and premature death. Early intervention to keep people in work and maintain social contacts can significantly reduce these costs.
>
> 3. Social isolation is an important risk factor for deteriorating mental health and suicide. Two-thirds of men under the age of 35 with mental health problems who die by suicide are unemployed.
>
> 4. Severe mental health problems, such as schizophrenia, are relatively rare, affecting around one in 200 adults each year.
>
> 5. GPs spend a third of their time on mental health issues. Prescription costs for anti-depressant drugs have risen significantly in recent years, and there are significant variations in access to talking therapies.
>
> 6. Carers themselves are twice as likely to have mental health problems if they provide substantial care. An estimated 6,000 to 17,000 children and young people care for an adult with mental health problems. (p 3)

The Academy of Medical Royal Colleges and Royal College of Psychiatrists' (2009) *No health without mental health* sees mental ill health as both a cause and a consequence of social exclusion and poverty. Severe mental ill health, which might result in admission to hospital, can lead to loss of employment or the disruption of a career path. As the OPDM (2004) report noted, there are numerous barriers that might prevent people getting back into the labour market and employment. Not least of these is the stigma attached to mental illness. While accepting that anyone from any social background or class can experience mental distress, the Marmot Review (2010) identifies a clear link between poverty, inequality and poor mental health. Those with the fewest resources are more likely to experience mental health problems. The question of causality remains a complex one, but as Murray (2016) notes, it is widely accepted that the impact of adverse life events – which surely must include living in poverty – are a factor in the development of mental health problems. Wilkinson and Pickett (2009) use the prevalence of mental distress as one of their measures for how a society functions, because the more unequal a society is, the greater the prevalence of mental distress.

There has been a series of excellent campaigns such as Time to Change (see www.time-to-change.org.uk), which seeks to challenge the stigma attached to mental illness. There is something of a paradox in broader societal attitudes to these issues. On the one hand, there is more open discussion about the nature of the problems. Every family in the country is touched in some way by these issues. However, there remains a level of shame and stigma. This is most apparent in the tabloid media – see, for example, Cummins (2013), on *The Sun*'s reporting of homicides. Social work on a professional level has a key role to play in challenging stereotypical and negative attitudes in this field.

It would be naive to fail to recognise that there has been a shift in societal attitudes – generally for the better. The observation that people can and do recover from serious mental health problems is, at first glance, a fairly uncontroversial statement. It reflects the fact that the recovery model, once at the margins of mental health, has become firmly established in the ethos of service provision. There are two recent excellent histories of mental health service provision. Scull's (2015) *Madness in civilisation* and Foot's (2015) *The man who closed the asylums* highlight the barriers that had to be overcome in the struggle to humanise mental health provision. Foot (2015) highlights the barriers that had to be overcome in the struggle to humanise mental health provision. Scull's study of societal responses to madness demonstrates that there appear to be few, if any, dignities that societies have not been prepared to inflict on citizens in the name of treatment. Foot's fascinating study of Franco Basaglia makes very clear the essential political nature of the structure and delivery of mental health care. The Recovery Model is based on several key assumptions. One of the most important is that people with mental health problems have to play a fundamental role as equal partners with mental health professionals in the design and delivery of services and support. The impacts of major mental illness are clearly social as they affect people's opportunities to work and, as discussed here, to establish social networks. There is a loop as this social marginalisation, by its nature, has potentially damaging impacts on an individual's mental health and sense of wellbeing. As

Newlin et al (2015) suggest, social work as a profession and discipline has social inclusion at its core. Social work practitioners support social inclusion on both an individual and organisational level.

The Recovery Model has been criticised from a radical standpoint, which sees its core values such as individualism and the focus on a return to work as a measure of recovery as too sympathetic or closely aligned with neoliberalism's key tropes. For example, Recovery in the Bin (RITB) – a user-led group – argues that the term 'recovery' has been colonised, and in that process, depoliticised. They set mental health in a much broader political and social context, as the following shows:

What we believe

We believe that the concept of "recovery" has been colonised by mental health services, commissioners and policy-makers.

We believe the growing development of this form of the "Recovery Model" is a symptom of neoliberalism, and that capitalism is at the root of the crisis! Many of us will never be able to "recover" living under these intolerable social and economic conditions, due to the effects of circumstances such as poor housing, poverty, stigma, racism, sexism, unreasonable work expectations, and countless other barriers.

We believe that the term "UnRecovered" is a valid and legitimate political self-definition (not a permanent description of anyone's mental state) and we emphasis its political and social contrast to "Recovered". This doesn't mean we want to remain "unwell" or "ill" but that we reject the new neoliberal intrusion on the word "recovery" that has been redefined, and taken over by market forces, humiliating treatment techniques and homogenising outcome measurements.

We believe that there are core principles of recovery that are worth saving, but that the colonisation of "recovery" undermines those principles which have so far championed autonomy and self-determination. These principles cannot be found in one-size-fits-all models, or calibrated by outcome measures. We also believe that autonomy and self-determination can only be attained through collective struggle rather than through individualistic striving and aspiration, as we are social beings.

> We propose to spread awareness of how neoliberalism and market forces shape the way mental health "recovery" is planned and delivered by services, including those within the voluntary sector. (RITB, no date)

The late lamented College of Social Work (TCSW) produced a curriculum guide for social work.

Good mental health has been defined as 'a state of wellbeing in which the individual realises his or her own abilities, can cope with the normal stresses of life, can work productively and fruitfully, and is able to make a contribution to his or her community' (WHO, 2014). RITB rightly highlights the dangers of these sorts of definitions in that they ignore fundamental questions such as what do we mean by 'can work productively and fruitfully', and 'make a contribution to his or her community'? These are inherently political questions. The advantage of such broad definitions is that they move us away from a deficit model approach. A social realist approach in the field of mental health recognises that mental distress is a reality, and acknowledges that it can have a powerful impact on individuals and their families. At the same time, such a perspective not only recognises but also foregrounds the impact of social factors including inequality and poverty. Such a critical perspective should also make social work practitioners aware of the ways that mental health services can reproduce and entrench inequality.

Work with refugees and asylum-seekers

Social work with refugees and asylum-seekers is one of the most challenging and complex areas of contemporary practice. There is not the space to examine all the issues and ethical dilemmas that are created here. Globalisation has led to the hyper-mobility of capital. This is also the case for those members of the financial elites and plutocracy (Milanovic, 2016). However, far from the new international moneyed elites, the movement of people escaping wars and political instability has become one of the most toxic of all political issues, one that has been exploited successfully by populist parties of the Right across Europe and the US in 2016. Social workers in particular, but not exclusively those working in the statutory sector, can be placed in very difficult ethical positions in this area. Humphries (2004a, 2004b) was extremely critical of the role of statutory social work in what she identified as the inhumanity of the asylum system. From this perspective, social workers had a professional and moral duty to challenge the essentially racist asylum and immigration systems, and there are clearly social workers doing this as part of local and national campaigns.

The history of humanity is a history of people moving across the globe. However, recent history has seen an increase in the movement of people. This has been brought about by a combination of globalisation, improved transportation and so on, and also increasing political instability. Asylum-seekers and refugees leave their homelands because they have been driven out by civil war, political instability and oppression (Gibney, 2004). The conditions that individuals and families endure in the process of seeking asylum are increasingly overlooked as the issues of migration are conflated with crime and terrorism. This is a technique that is exemplified by the Leave Campaign's infamous poster. It used a photograph of Syrian refugees queuing at the border, portraying them as some of the 70 million Turks who would allegedly come to the UK in the unlikely event that Turkey ever joined the EU. The racist discourse around immigration is not a new feature of British public life.

The current international law relating to claiming asylum is part of the system that was established after the horrors of the Second World War. The right to claim asylum is a right enshrined in Article 14 of the Universal Declaration of Human Rights of 1948 and the 1951 UN Convention on the Status of Refugees. This is an important statement as it reminds us that the UK, along with other countries, is a signatory to international treaties that establish these obligations. Despite these long-standing duties, asylum has become a toxic political issue. Fell and Fell (2013) note that the social work response has not been planned on a strategic level, with the Social Care Institute for Excellence (SCIE) only producing a good practice guide in 2010. This appears quite shocking given the importance of the issue, including the potential vulnerabilities of asylum-seekers. It also seems to be at odds with its political significance.

This book is concerned with how social work and social workers should respond to the issues of poverty and the potential impacts it has on the lives of those who uses services. It has also examined the processes of 'Othering'. These are both crucial factors in the lives of asylum-seekers. Despite the horrors that they have had to endure, the tabloid media has maintained a level of vitriolic attack on asylum-seekers that panders to racist and fascist ideologies that see other groups as 'sub-human' (Omonira-Oyekanmi, 2014a, 2014b). Prior to the Immigration and Asylum Act 1999, asylum-seekers had limited access to welfare benefits. The Act established a new, extremely harsh and punitive welfare system for those seeking asylum – the National

Asylum Support Service (NASS). This was, in part, a populist New Labour response to the notion that the over-generous welfare system attracted asylum-seekers. The main features of the Act were that asylum-seekers were largely not allowed to work and were paid benefits in vouchers that were only redeemable at certain shops. The level of benefit was at 70 per cent of the rate of Income Support – below a minimum level that the government thought was acceptable for UK citizens. The Children's Society (2012) highlighted the impact of this benefit policy. Their analysis showed that asylum-seekers with children were struggling to meet their basic needs because of these policies. NASS also operates a 'dispersal' system whereby asylum-seekers who are not immediately detained at ports are sent to accommodation throughout the country. There is no choice in this system. When it was introduced, asylum-seekers were often sent to deprived areas where existing pressures on services meant that there was an increase in racial tensions (Robinson et al, 2003).

The question then is, how can social work as a profession and individual workers develop a humane model of practice given the policy constraints and the increasingly hostile nature of public debate about these issues? Fell and Fell (2013), influenced by the philosophical approach of Kant, Levinas and Derrida, argue that humane and effective practice can take place in this field. It is situated in the voluntary sector. They note that it would be foolish and insulting to pretend that the legal and policy system does not exist – and that it is a harsh one. However, this is a very different proposition that sees social workers as exercising immigration controls.

Fell and Fell's (2013) model is represented in Figure 5.2.

Figure 5.2: A social work process with asylum-seekers

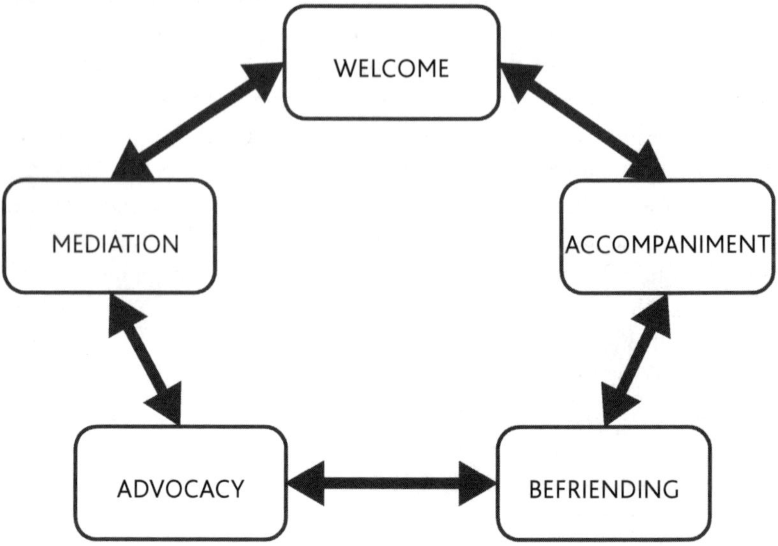

Source: Fell and Fell (2013)

These are elements that will be recognisable from other areas of social work practice but come together here to show that there is a challenge to the broader narrative. There are many – individuals, community groups, church organisations, political groups and other organisations – who do not subscribe to the 'Othering' agenda and who are prepared to offer their help.

Conclusion

Webb (2010) argues that social work is often defended on the grounds that it is a 'public good'. It performs a necessary role in supporting and protecting vulnerable people. This is one aspect of the role. Webb (2010) also suggests that social work has a redistributive function. It is funded by general taxation, and the majority of contributors will not use the services, or will only do so for short periods. Social work can also play a role in building social capital and networks. The enhancement of these is in the interests of all citizens. If we examine Wilkinson and Pickett's (2009) societal measures of physical health, mental health, drug abuse, education, imprisonment, obesity, social mobility, trust and community life, violence, teenage pregnancies and child wellbeing, we can see that they are linked to poverty and deprivation, and also that there is a potential role for social work in the alleviating their effects. The three areas discussed in this chapter highlight the importance of addressing such issues based on ecological approaches.

The huge political, economic and cultural changes that form the backdrop to the issues discussed in this book have left many social workers feeling isolated and under siege (White, 2009). It should be noted that these issues are also ones that have had an impact on social work education. Far from being exempt from audit and bureaucratic cultures, universities seem to have enthusiastically embraced NPM. The issues that are highlighted as sources of frustration for social work practitioners – increasing bureaucratic demands, lack of direct work with people, a culture of targets and on occasions a macho management culture – are all present in different forms in higher education. In addition, there has been a series of somewhat crude attempts to portray social work educators as a group of political radicals. This was most apparent during Michael Gove's tenure as Secretary of State for Education. In 2013 he attacked the 'dogma' that he saw as dominating social work training. In a speech to the NSPCC, he argued that idealistic students are misled about the nature of the work that they will undertake:

> They will be encouraged to see these individuals as victims of social injustice whose fate is overwhelmingly decreed by the economic forces and inherent inequalities which scar our society. This analysis is, sadly, as widespread as it is pernicious. It robs individuals of the power of agency and breaks the link between an individual's actions and the consequences. It risks explaining away substance abuse, domestic violence and personal irresponsibility, rather than doing away with them. Social workers overly influenced by this analysis not only rob families of a proper sense of responsibility, they also abdicate their own. (Gove, 2013, np)

Hidden within this are some elements that the main thrust of the analysis presented here would support – for example, the danger that an over-reliance on a structural analysis will ignore or diminish individual agency. However, the rest is based on a false assumption. Social work education has not focused on structural explanations. It is largely dominated by what could be termed psycho-dynamic approaches.

Gove also commissioned a report from Sir Martin Narey about social work education. Narey's report, which was based on a series of interviews, was highly critical of social work education. Its focus was on children and families' social work, but some of its criticisms were clearly made more broadly. It argued that social work courses were not academically rigorous – ironically, Narey's report was heavily criticised for its flawed, that is, non-existent, methodology. This was part of a series of attacks on social work education. In 2014, in an interview with *The Guardian*, Alan Jones, the president of the Association of Directors of Children's Services (ADCS), told the paper he was fed up with 'all these academics turning out crap social workers writing to *The Guardian*.' This not surprisingly led to a backlash. The interview was about the potential outsourcing of child protection social work, so has to be seen in that context – presenting the alleged failure of public services as justification for privatisation. It also disappointingly, but perhaps not surprisingly, plays to a series of stereotypes about social workers, academics in general, and social work academics in particular. Jones subsequently apologised for the language used, but not, significantly, for the thrust of his comments.

It is argued throughout this book that poverty should be understood as the result of structural forces. This is not to deny that there are individual factors at play. The 'othering' underclass discourse portrays poverty as the outcomes of the moral failings of individuals, communities and groups. The acknowledgement that poverty is a structural issue presents social work and social workers with a dilemma, as most social work is still practiced following a casework model or some variant of it. Community social work that was actually promoted by the Seebohm Report (1968) as a desired model struggles to maintain a foothold. Pierson (2008) suggests five blocks to tackling what he termed 'social exclusion':

- maximising income and securing basic resources
- strengthening social supports and networks
- working in partnership
- creating channels for effective participation
- focusing on neighbourhood and community practice

This approach has an intrinsic appeal because of its ecological focus. It combines social work's traditional focus and concern with individuals and families, but uses this as a base from which to develop broader community responses. Both elements are required for effective social work practice. It is an approach to practice that imagines that there is a continuum that ranges from individual to community-based approaches. Both ends of the continuum are fatally flawed. A solely individualistic approach ignores the community or social circumstances in which that person is living. Logically, it casts aside issues such as class, gender, race and sexual orientation. It also has to ignore social and political history. For example, any understanding of the experiences of young black men in mental health services that ignored historical factors and current inequalities would be totally inadequate. At the other end of this continuum is a danger that individual experiences as well as strengths and resilience are ignored by mechanistic explanations.

The Professional Capabilities Framework (PCF) domains should be viewed in totality rather than as a series of separate entities. For example, values and ethics have to be seen to underpin all approaches to social work practice. Part of the concern about the advent of managerialism is that it has the potential to strip social work of its ethical dimensions, and creates situations in which practitioners feel they have lost professional autonomy. In concluding this chapter, I argue that the PCF can form the basis for a re-engagement with the social justice dimension of social work practice. I should make it clear here that I do not dispute that for individual practitioners this has always been the case. My argument is that the practice environment makes it increasingly difficult for social workers to carve out the creative and professional space to do that. There is a strange dichotomy between work like the Narey report that suggests we need social workers who have a greater level of professional competence, and the creation of a practice environment that is ultimately deskilling and process-driven.

The PCF was originally developed by the Social Work Reform Board as part of the overview of the profession following the death of 'Baby P'. The PCF:

- Sets out consistent expectations of social workers at every stage in their career
- Provides a backdrop to both initial social work education and continuing professional development after qualification
- Informs the design and implementation of the national career structure
- Gives social workers a framework around which to plan their careers and professional development. (www.basw.co.uk/pcf/)

The PCF is divided into nine domains. Domain 4 is 'Rights and justice'. The PCF contains a very clear statement that at all stages of their professional career and development, from entry to the profession onwards, that social workers 'understand the effects of oppression, discrimination and poverty.' The ethic and value base of the profession thus includes an explicit statement that acknowledges the role and impact of poverty in the lives of service users. The PCF is divided into levels as well as domains. These include end of first placement, final placement and the ASYE (Assessed and Supported Year in Employment). At all of these levels it is a requirement that social work students and newly qualified staff 'Recognise the impact of poverty and social exclusion and promote enhanced economic status through access to education, work, housing, health services and welfare benefits' (www.basw.co.uk/pcf/).

At the level of experienced social worker there is an expectation that they will be able to 'Support others to enable individuals to access opportunities that may enhance their economic status (eg education, work, housing, health services and welfare benefits)' (www.basw. co.uk/pcf/).

The PCF thus makes anti-poverty social work a key requirement of professional development and progression. The question is how students can demonstrate their commitment to these values and ideas in a practical sense. I feel that the starting point for this has to be social work education. Gove-ites may believe that social work education has focused for too long on structural explanations of poverty. I have to say that my experience across social work academia, including teaching, reviewing journal articles, attending social work conferences and external examining, is that the exact opposite is the case. Debates about poverty and class certainly appear dotted about the social work curricula. The notion that social work education focuses on this to the exclusion of psychological theory does not seem plausible to me. The result is that the social and community context in which individuals and families live their lives is often missing from assessments. This may be because it is easier to engage with issues on an individual level rather than feeling overwhelmed by the need for huge political changes that are unlikely to take place. There are, of course, those who would seek to deny the reality that social work and the nature of welfare services in their broadest sense are fundamentally political questions. Gupta (2015) refers to poverty as the 'elephant in the room' of children and families' social work, the key factor in the increase in neglect cases that is never openly acknowledged as playing a contributory factor in so many areas.

Using the PCF as a basis for examining how social workers can respond to and help to tackle poverty, I argue, can lead to the development of a particular model of social work practice. It should start from a rejection of the pathologising discourses of the 'poor'. This has been a consistent feature of social work since the modern development of the profession. Its continued existence has been examined at length in Chapter 3. The PCF stands as the basis for the development of a practice that is committed to social justice – both in individual day-to-day work, and also for the profession to engage, as it has always sought to do, in progressive campaigns. Practice should be based on ecological rather than narrow individualistic approaches, it should also be community-focused and orientated towards developing existing and building social capital. In the processes there is a need for practice based on relational social work and an ethic of care. These methods are underpinned by recognition of the inherent worth of all individuals, which requires a rebuilding of a social state. It is to that we turn in the next chapter.

SIX

Reimagining a social state

In this chapter, I explore potential alternative ethical and philosophical approaches that can be used to develop an alternative model of welfare, citizenship and social provision. The current economic crisis provides, counter-intuitively, an opportunity for social work and social workers to challenge the orthodoxy of a focus on risk management. This chapter is therefore concerned with exploring a route out of this mire. I argue that there needs to be a fundamental shift in the approach to the practice of social work, that this will lead to a reconnection with social work practice based on relational approaches.

In this area, the work of the late French philosopher Emmanuel Levinas can be used as a starting point to examine the notions of the duties we, as humans, owe each other. I have argued that the underclass discourse and the stigmatising representation of the poor and poor neighbourhoods have to be seen as a form of 'Othering'. In addition, social work has been involved in these processes. Levinas's work is a rejoinder to these approaches and a call for humanistic values based on mutual recognition. Sayer (2005a, 2005b, 2015) makes a very persuasive argument that class, poverty and inequality have to be approached as fundamentally moral issues. As a profession, social work needs to discover new forms of community and individual engagement. This is not simply an argument for the return of a paternalistic form of casework, even if it is in a modernised form. An alternative ethical framework that combines insights from the philosophers Martha Fineman, Amartya Sen, Martha Nussbaum and Emmanuel Levinas can act as the basis for an approach that places human dignity at the heart of social work practice. This has to be seen as part of a wider process that recasts the relationship between the individual and the state. In particular, it requires that social work is less complicit in the processing of 'Othering'.

How can social work make this shift? It might seem perverse, but it can look to the cracks that have occurred in the US penal state and a Supreme Court decision for inspiration. In *Brown vs Plata*, a group of prisoners successfully sued the state of California, arguing that the state's penal policies, the overcrowding they produced and the resultant inadequate healthcare amounted to a breach of the eighth amendment of the constitution prohibiting cruel and unusual punishment. In deciding the case in favour of the prisoners, Justice Kennedy stated that 'prisoners retain the essence of human dignity' (*Brown, et al vs Plata et al*, 563 U.S. 493, 2011). Their treatment did not recognise this. I argue that we need to return to a culture that sees the poor, marginalised and excluded not as sites of risk, but as fellow citizens. The dominant risk paradigm leads to a form of practice that is mired in bureaucracy. This creates barriers to the establishment of positive working relationships between social workers and service users. There is a gap between the rhetoric of partnership working, choice and empowerment' and the reality of practice where social workers spend less time working directly with people. This is a source of widespread professional frustration but it is also, I argue, a recipe for poor social work practice. Munro (2011) highlighted that child protection is highly complex work that requires professionals to make tough decisions. This is true for the profession as a whole. Her report also indicated that social workers needed more autonomy, not less. Here I argue that this requires not just organisational change, but that cultural attitudes within agencies also have to shift. Rediscovering dignity is a starting point for this process.

As I am writing this in 2016, the radio news is reporting that Thomas Mair has been found guilty of the brutal politically motivated murder of Labour MP Jo Cox. Mair, a neo-Nazi, with links to far-Right groups in the UK and a fascination with Nazi Germany and Apartheid South Africa, murdered Ms Cox days before the EU referendum. The news of Mair's conviction is another chapter in the tumultuous political history of 2016. It is a year in which the progressive inclusive values that form the bedrock of social work have been under attack in many ways. Jo Cox was not a social worker, but in her charity work, local constituency work and campaigning on issues such as the plight of Syrian refuges she embodied what should be the core values of the profession. Her murder, in the context of the Brexit 'Leave' campaign, which appealed to racism of the most basic kind, is clearly a personal tragedy and a cataclysmic event for her family and loved ones. It is also an attack on the principles of a pluralist, liberal democracy that she, in her fundamental decency and humanity, represented. Her statement in her maiden speech that "we are far more united and have far more in common with each other than things that divide us" is an expression of the core values that we need to rediscover.

The politics of discourses of human rights and dignity

The UN Declaration of Human Rights states in Article 1 that 'All human beings are born free and equal in dignity and rights' (United

Nations General Assembly, 1948). Habermas (2010) notes that the language and modern legal framework of human rights legislation has developed in response to the atrocities and oppression of Nazism and the Gulag. These abuses of human rights are violations of human dignity. Thus it is only through a common set of moral values that recognise the equal dignity of all human beings that legal protections against their violation that rights can be established. The discourse of dignity has become a prominent one in legal and judicial decision-making (Denniger, cited in Habermas, 2010). This discourse is not restricted to the legal sphere; it is also a key component in broader ethical discussions that overlap with the law – bio-ethics and end-of-life care being two clear examples. This modern notion is a recasting of Kant's (1996) categorical imperative that every person should be viewed as an 'end in themselves'. This approach is in contrast to utilitarianism and other forms of consequentialism.

The post-Second World War notion of dignity is contrasted by Habermas (2010) with the 19th-century development of the liberal rights of freedom of association and religion, protections against arbitrary arrest, and so on. These so-called democratic rights of participation or classical civil rights were a buffer to prevent the intrusion of the state into the private sphere. It should be noted here that these rights, despite their egalitarian and universal rhetoric, were not enjoyed by all – women and minorities being two obvious examples of groups not included. The current notion of dignity has at its root an explicit egalitarianism that does not allow for exclusion – unless one regards certain groups of people as non-human, this is a logical fallacy. Habermas (2010) argues that any appeal to current human rights discourse is based on a concept of human dignity. The outrage at the abuse of political prisoners, the use of torture and the treatment of asylum-seekers and immigrants is the result of a response to the humiliations that these violations of human dignity entail. These may be physical indignities and humiliations such as the photographs of naked Iraqi prisoners at Abu Ghraib (Hersh, 2004), or the psychological impact of asylum-seekers being made to wear identifying wristbands (Taylor, 2016). We are outraged or should be because of our shared humanity and recognition that we have obligations to others.

The experience of living in poverty is an exclusionary one. In these terms, it is an abuse of individual and community dignity and thus an issue of human rights. Rawls (1971) argued that the classical civil rights of political liberalism only acquire equal value for citizens when they are accompanied by social and cultural rights. Rawls' concern with social inequalities meant that he saw a danger in whole groups being effectively excluded from the broader society and culture. Fraser (1995, 2010) sees dignity as the fundamental basis for the equal respect of citizens. Fraser argues that the claim for equal treatment on the basis of identity must have within it a simultaneous claim for redistribution for it to have value. Sayer (2005a, 2005b) suggests that in seeing poverty as a moral issue, it is important to note that it has been largely excluded from these claims to equality based on identity. 'Poor' is not an identity that is claimed or celebrated in the same way as other modern social and political identities (Fraser, 1995). In fact, as we saw in Chapter 3, any claims that individuals or groups in modern liberal democracies are poor are quite often dismissed out of hand. This is part of the process of silencing and marginalising groups or individuals. The challenge to the oppression of women and racial and sexual minorities has involved a challenge to stereotypical constructions of identity. These have, of course, been led by members of those groups. This appears much more problematic in the area of poverty.

Dworkin (1995) notes that dignity is both a powerful but also a vague concept. This is part of its attraction, but also, perhaps, part of its weakness. Dworkin also added that any notion of human rights had to accept that dignity would be at its core. The modern – by modern I mean post-Second World War – concept of human dignity is described as 'a value which is held universally and applies to all human beings' (Misztal, 2013 p 102). As she notes, this concept of dignity has been the driver of recent political events such as the Arab Spring and Black Lives Matter. However, the roots of the notion can be found in the Greek and Roman Stoics. Sandel (2009) argues that justice requires that all human beings are afforded rights because they are human beings and thus capable of Kantian reason. It also a key idea in major world religions. For example, Catholic social teaching holds that humans are afforded special status because they are created in God's image. The modern use of dignity has developed from a notion that was associated with rank and status to a universalist approach. Thus dignity is afforded because of one's status as a human being (Waldron, 2007). In this sense, the notion of dignity can act as a link or a bridge between the individual and wider society (Berger, 1970). Kateb (2011) argues that in this approach dignity is based on the notion that every individual is equal, and that no species is equal to human beings. This argument is actually counter to recent technological and other developments that question our fundamental notions of humanity (Rose, 2007; Fuller, 2011). For radical ethicists, Kateb (2011) excludes animals. We now know that, genetically, primates are our relations. It is therefore argued that logically we owe them the duties that we owe humans (Singer, 2006).

There are two broad objections to the notion of human dignity and the discourse of human rights as outlined above. The first echoes Dworkin (1995) in claiming that dignity is a vague concept, but then goes on to reject its use on this basis. Pinker (2008) dismisses the use of the notion. He suggests that dignity 'is a squishy, subjective notion, hardly up to the heavyweight moral demands assigned to it' (p 1). Bioethicist Macklin (2003) argued that the term was being used to block rather than further research. She suggested that 'Dignity is a useless concept' (p 1419). In the ethical field it can be replaced by autonomy as this inevitably leads to the conclusion that research can only be carried out with the informed consent of participants. This would clearly exclude Mengele's experiments on Jewish people during the Second World War and other medical scandals such as the withholding of treatment in the Tuskegee syphilis case. In the Tuskegee case, African-American men were denied treatment with penicillin even though it had been established that this was effective (Brandt, 1978). Macklin suggests that once you recognise autonomy, then dignity adds nothing. However, a notion of autonomy surely stems from recognition of an individual's basic humanity – a key aspect of the idea of dignity. In both the Mengele and Tuskegee cases, the 'experiments' took place on individuals who were members of groups, legally, socially and culturally defined as lacking the full rights of liberal citizenship, that is, those not treated with dignity.

The second challenge to the notion of the human rights discourse is most forthrightly expressed in the work of the radical French philosopher, Alain Badiou. He remains strongly committed to the ideas of the 1968 movement that challenged the key notions of Western liberal capitalist democracies. His critique of capitalism sees it not as a progressive force that led to the establishment of liberal rights, but as a form of nihilism (Badiou, 2015). In his discussion of the Badiouian critique of the human rights discourse, Webb (2009) notes that social work makes a number of claims in this area. The first is that it claims to be a profession that is concerned, one might add, uniquely concerned, with questions of human rights. This a popular claim – among social workers at least, and it has two main effects. It is an inherent claim of moral superiority over other professional value bases, and it also claims to imbue social work practice with an unchallenged ethical base. I would argue that this is at best naive, but at worst dangerously complacent, ignoring the involvement of social work and individual social workers in clear abuses of human rights. It can also act as a default position that argues that social work somehow brings a uniquely ethical different perspective to practice. Mental health social work is an excellent example where Badiou argues that modern discourse, based as it is on individualism, is actually an adjunct to neoliberalism.

Webb (2009) outlines the ways in which modern social work ethics reflect the post-modern turn and its concern with identity, diversity and difference. The result is that identity has replaced class as the marker of oppression. This is clearly not an attack on the progress that has been made in the area of social and other legislation relating to the position of minorities. It is a concern that a discursive narrative of inequality masks the fundamental nature of modern society where economic resources are concentrated in a small elite. Webb (2009) concludes that social work has shifted from a concern with inequality to a focus on broader issues of marginalisation. For Badiou, these notions lead to a conflict between an expressed universalism derived from Kant and Habermas, and respect for the Other. The result is that Western liberalism will only respect what it sees as acceptable forms of difference.

An example of this sort of thinking is the idea that the US 2001 invasion of Afghanistan was part of a feminist project concerned with the rights of women. Bunting (2011) notes that women's rights were subsumed into the War on Terror – an unlikely alliance. Badiou (2015) sees human rights discourse as essentially duplicitous – human rights are accorded to those who best fit the Western liberal ideal. From this radical perspective, the politics of human rights leads to a new form of US-led imperialism in international politics. On the domestic front, a mixture of communitarianism and identity politics leads to the marginalisation of class-based claims for redistribution.

The politics of 2016 in both the UK and US, alongside broader developments, seem to mark a retreat from the development of the sort of universal and international forms of civic cohesion that Habermas (2010) envisages emerging from the broader human rights discourse. The turbulent world of 2016 has seen as a retreat into or a return to a politics that is essentialist in response to issues of race, gender and sexuality. The fact that the most high-profile proponents of this politics – Trump and Farage – revelled, personally and politically, in this challenge to the alleged liberal orthodoxy seems to add to rather than detract from their wider appeal. There is a danger of falling into a self-defeating pessimism in response to some of these developments. This would undo or perhaps fail to defend the progress that has been made in terms of civil, political and social rights for members of minority groups. It also seems to take as given that the current situation is one that will not change. One more optimistic approach lies in the field of cosmopolitanism (Appiah, 2007). This philosophy argues that human beings are members of a single community that is based on a shared morality.

Levinas, the Other and social work

The Other

Before exploring Levinas' work in more depth and its relevance for social work, we need to examine the notion of the 'Other'. Webb (2009) has outlined the ways in which social work ethics over the past 30 years have increasingly focused on challenging notions of the Other. Othering is the process by which individuals or groups are cast into a subordinate or inferior social position. They are 'Other' – not one of the dominant groups. Said's (1978) classic examination of the Western cultural representations of the East – Asia, North Africa and the Middle East – Orientalism – has been hugely influential in the development of post-colonial studies. It examines the ways in which dominant cultures represent images of subaltern populations as a means of reproducing and reinforcing the power of the colonising peoples. Said identifies three separate but related elements in these processes, the outcome of which is the creation of the Other. These are as follows:

- Homogenisation: the rich cultural diversity of the areas under discussion is dismissed or overlooked – all Oriental people are the same
- Feminisation: an East/West binary is established and Oriental people are lesser
- Essentialism: people are reduced from complexity to a series of innate, racially ascribed, characteristics

Critical theory applies these insights to the development of attitudes to sexual and other minorities. These subaltern narratives of colonised oppression are clearly not accepted without challenge by oppressed peoples. Identities are complex, changing and not fixed. There are many examples where radical figures, for example, Malcolm X (Marable, 2011), have rejected or subverted imposed identities as part of creating a new revolutionary one.

Sayer (2005b) notes that part of the process of minorities challenging discrimination has been the demanding of group recognition or the claiming of an identity as legitimate. This involves undermining a pathologised identity and then recasting it or reclaiming it as a legitimate one. He goes on to argue that class, unlike, for example, ethnicity, has not been subject to such identity claims. Class stands apart from these other forms of identity. Disadvantages attached to lower-class status are not the result of misrecognition or a failure to value identity; they are the result of fundamental inequalities.

Fraser uses the term 'misrecognition' to refer to the practices by which individuals or groups are excluded from political, social and economic processes.

> The most general meaning of justice is parity of participation. According to this radical-democratic interpretation of the principle of equal moral worth, justice requires social arrangements that permit all to participate as peers in social life. Overcoming injustice means dismantling institutionalized obstacles that prevent some people from participating on a par with others, as full partners in social interaction. Previously, I have analysed two distinct kinds of obstacles to participatory parity, which correspond to two distinct species of injustice. On the one hand, people can be impeded from full participation by economic structures that deny them the resources they need in order to interact with others as peers; in that case they suffer from distributive injustice or maldistribution. On the other hand, people can also be prevented from interacting on terms of parity by institutionalized hierarchies of cultural value that deny them the requisite standing; in that case they suffer from status inequality or misrecognition. (Fraser, 2007, p 20)

Both Fraser and Sayer note that there has been more progress in challenging 'institutionalised hierarchies of cultural value' than other areas. It should be emphasised that it is not being suggested that these processes have been totally successful or that they are complete. Sayer (2005b) highlights the process of moral boundary drawing whereby groups represent difference in terms of moral worth. The underclass discourse is a prime example of these processes. Sayer (2005b, 2015) concludes that economic distribution has no connection to moral worth. The biggest determining factor remains who your parents are, and this is clearly not an indicator of any moral qualities you have. It is purely a matter of luck.

In Chapter 3 we examined some of the stigma that remains attached to class and lower-class positions. Savage et al (2001) note that, certainly in the UK context, class remains a 'loaded moral signifier'. Sayer (2005b) argues that the experience of class still revolves around notions of shame. However, these experiences are often individualised in the UK context, so that the issue is presented as an individual failing rather than a challenge to structural inequalities – 'he or she has a chip on their shoulder' – or as a legitimate expression of grievance (Reay, 2005). Similar terms and phrases have also been used about members of minority ethnic groups. The exploration of notions of class has been closely examined in the fields of political science, where it is seen as a key factor in patterns of voting. A more psychosocial approach needs to be developed to examine the potential damage of symbolic violence, that is, 'the violence which is exercised upon a social agent with his or her complicity' (Bourdieu and Wacquant, 1992, p 108).

The work of Emmanuel Levinas

There has been an increasing interest in the work of the late French Lithuanian philosopher Emmanuel Levinas (1906–95) and its possible application to the world of social work practice. Levinas' work is concerned with the nature of the face-to-face encounter. He argues that Husserl's phenomenology lacks one of the key elements – the intersubjective nature of life. The work of Levinas, a Talmudic scholar, is complex, but one of its key themes is encapsulated in the idea expressed by fellow Holocaust survivor, Elie Wiesel, that:

> We must not see any person as an abstraction. Instead, we must see in every person a universe with its own secrets, with its own treasures, with its own sources of anguish, and with some measure of triumph. (Wiesel, 1992, p 1)

The traditional approach in Western philosophy has been that ethical positions are derived from knowledge. Levinas turns this proposition on its head. Ethics, for Levinas (1999, 2005), must precede knowledge. At the core of Levinas' work is the description of face-to-face contact with the Other. He argues that it is in this process that we generate ethics. The Other here is a translation of the French word *autrui*, which means 'the other person', 'someone else' (that is, other than oneself). Levinas argues that we should avoid what he terms 'totalities'. Rossiter (2011), in her discussion of the application of Levinas to social work practice, suggests that totalities can be viewed as the belief systems through which we conceptualise. We use a whole range of totalities to understand individuals before we actually have any social interaction with them. These systems are, of course, incomplete and limiting, but remain very attractive. It must be said that social work, despite protestations to the contrary, remains very attached to a whole raft of totalities, but also critical of others who use them. For Levinas, there is a danger or tension in the clash between the cultural power of totalities and the singularity of the Face that we encounter. Our representations of people are always incomplete. Individuals are always much more complex and have more roles or identities than our systems of representation allow. In sociological terms, Hall (2003) argued that individuals have increasingly complex narratives of identity because of the changing nature of society.

Rossiter (2011) outlines the potential attraction of the Levinasian approach to social work. It appeals to traditional social work notions that seek to set aside stereotypical representation. There is a danger that the radical aspects of Levinas' thought are missed if his ideas are viewed as a call to respect individuals. Rossiter (2011) argues that his work can form the basis for what she terms 'unsettled practice'. This results from a tension between the need for representation and its impact on individuals – in Levinas' terms, totalising representations of people required for claims of justice to be made. However, at the same time, these representations are forms of symbolic violence. Perpich (2008) argues that these tensions are played out in the face-to-face encounter. This is an area that is of key interest to social work as, despite the bureaucratisation of the profession, it is still in these sorts of encounters that most social work takes place. It is also the overwhelming motivating factor for social workers and students joining the profession. For Levinas, the face of the Other is an explicit call to recognise the uniqueness of individuals and to not fall prey to a pre-existing image or conception. Butler (2004, p 145) concludes that 'a loss of the human' takes place when it is 'captured by the image'.

Rossiter (2011) suggests that one of the practical applications of Levinas's approach in social work would be to avoid the use of 'totalised knowledge'. This is clearly a challenge in the modern social work world as the pressures on systems and practitioners mean that approaches are increasingly reductionist. An approach influenced by Levinas would reject some of the totalities of modern social work. I am thinking here of the toxic trio, disorganised attachments and other forms of jargon that have become the lingua franca of practice. The difficulty with these approaches is not the underpinning theoretical ideas. These are a matter of the theoretical bent of the individual practitioner. Social work always has practitioners who come from a range of theoretical perspectives. It is the dominance of these perspectives and also the way that they restrict that raises concern. They act as a barrier to the establishment of genuine relationships. Time pressures and the demands of bureaucracy make it even more difficult for practitioners to establish, develop and maintain relationships. Rossiter (2011) argues that any representations of a service user cannot possibly capture the singularity of that individual. The danger is that the service user becomes an extension or projection of the social worker's knowledge. For Levinas (1999), this is the symbolic murder of the Other. Thus 'totalities' can become a dangerous social work shorthand. From this perspective, social work totalities – looked-after child, mental health service user or victim of domestic violence – are ultimately as damaging and limiting as any others. This is the fundamental challenge of Levinas' ethical position and approach. It is one, however, that should be attractive to social workers as it has so much in common with the profession's expressed ethical position.

Martha Fineman and the vulnerable subject

The American feminist and legal scholar wrote 'The vulnerable subject: anchoring equality in the human condition' (Fineman, 2008). In it she argues that there is a need for a more equal and responsive state. Fineman argues that vulnerability is a universal and constant feature of the human condition. The starting point for the development of a more responsive state has to be an acknowledgement of this. Vulnerable people should be the focus of the policies that states develop as this would result in greater equality. Fineman (2004) argues that current policies start from the position or assumption of an imagined autonomous individual. She suggests that autonomy is a myth – we all need or will need some care at some point in our lives. No one would make it to adulthood without the support of other members of society.

Fineman notes that we tend to emphasise capacity, independence or autonomy. This is certainly the case in social work. The term 'vulnerability' is used within social work, but I think that it is not used in the same sense that Fineman used it. In social work practice, it becomes an almost all-encompassing term that can be used as a justification for intervention. It is paternalistic. In Fineman's work, it is the basis for a mutual understanding or reciprocity. The focus on individualism ignores or seeks to set aside these basic conditions of mutuality that are required for social systems to function. This is particularly the case in the provision of care, 'care' being used in its broadest sense here. Current systems privatise our collective responsibility for care. Fineman is writing in the US context, where there has never been a welfare state of the post-war social democratic style that neoliberalism so opposes. However, the arguments she presents are increasingly relevant to the

European context where the social contract is under increasing, and possibly terminal, pressure.

Vulnerability is different for different people because of different positions in a complex web of economic and institutional relationships. This position is not simply a question of economic power and capital. It also reflects social, cultural and historical factors. The social institutions and organisations that surround us provide us with a range of assets such as material wealth and property. All of us are vulnerable and dependent on others to exist. By failing to acknowledge our common vulnerability, Fineman argues, we lose sight of the ways in which power and privilege operate, providing support and protection to the wealthiest members of society. These protections are not available to more marginalised members of society. – we need to examine the sort of support the richest receive.

Fineman argues that in the current model, the state is what she terms 'a restrained state'. The notion of the private (family) serves as a significant psychological, cultural and legal barrier, which keeps the state out of institutions and activities.

This makes ensuring equality more difficult. The state has been prevented from acting as the principal monitor of an equal society. Fineman argues that the current state and formal policies of equality have failed to achieve their aims. Formal legal equality does not:

- protect against subordination and domination
- protect against all forms of discrimination – for example, on grounds of sexual orientation or disability.
- formal equality policies are based on the existing allocations of resources and power
- such policies do not hold the state accountable

The state faces a clear obligation not to privilege to any group of citizens. There remains a deeply entrenched cultural norm that people are autonomous. They do not need to depend on anyone else. Dependency is seen as a weakness. This is despite the fact that it is actually unavoidable. Fineman concludes that society should be egalitarian. In a more egalitarian society, the state would and should be more responsive. Fineman's work can be part of a shift in attitudes in these areas and of reclaiming the social sphere. The attraction for social work is that this is clearly an egalitarian ethos. In addition, it calls for a reinvigoration of the public provision of care as the privatisation of this sphere serves to entrench already existing inequalities. There is a danger that the use of the term 'vulnerable' becomes subsumed in a culture that limits rather than extends rights.

The Capabilities Approach

The Capabilities Approach (CA) was developed by the work of Sen and Nussbaum. It was originally focused on the issues of poverty in the Global South. It is a rights-based approach that can be used as an alternative to a model that is solely based on income as a measure of human welfare. The economic, social, political and cultural dimensions of life are recognised within the model. Sen outlines five dimensions to the assessment of capability:

- The importance of social and political freedoms – for example, a totalitarian system by its very nature restricts the capabilities of most of its citizens.
- Individual differences mean that there are variations between citizens in the ability to transform resources into valuable activities – this leads to concerns with issues such as fair access.
- Happiness is the result of many factors, not simply wealth or position.
- Evaluating human welfare requires the consideration of a range of factors. Some of these are materialistic and some are not – for example, freedom of expression or religion. There is a focus on the importance of the civil society.
- There is a need for a fairer distribution of opportunities within society.

Current economic structures mean that people have equal opportunities to realise or achieve their capabilities. These issues call for governments and also institutions to play a much more active role in creating an environment where citizens have more equal opportunities, which means greater investment in public services, for example. One of the impacts of austerity has been that the realm of the public good has been increasingly restricted. Cuts in local services have a disproportionate impact on the poorest. A good example of this is the closure of libraries – middle-class or wealthier individuals are able to access these facilities in the private sphere online. The CA offers an alternative model to the current reconstruction of poverty as a form of moral failure. It acknowledges the role of agency as well as the structural limitations of the individual exercise of it.

Marian Barnes' ethic of care

One of the recurring themes of this book is that neoliberalism attempts to marketise all of human activity to marginalise some of the key aspects that make us human – social solidarity, love, respect and notions of humanity dignity. This is readily apparent in the area of social care. By reducing it to a commodity, this then serves to rob it of its wider social value. The results are all around us in the current provision of services – and adult social care is a particularly illuminating but depressing example. The privatising process has led to a situation where carers doing this vital work experience some of the worst pay and conditions – pressures to make more visits in a shorter time, lack of holiday and sick pay and so on. Barnes (2006) argues that the philosophical base of the caring relationship has been sacrificed on the altar of bureaucracy and managerialism. She identifies five underlying moral principles that can underpin an ethics of care:

1. Attentiveness
2. Responsibility
3. Competence
4. Responsiveness
5. Trust

These principles are clearly compatible with social work professional values, and point towards a relational rather than a functional or bureaucratic relationship. They stand in contrast to the more managerialist approaches that have been outlined earlier in the book. I would argue that these key principles can be applied across the whole domain of social work practice. There may well be certain areas where their operationalisation may be more complex and demanding – for example child protection work. However, all social work has at its core a concern with building mutually respectful relationships of support. This can and should be the case even when intervening in the most challenging areas. It must be possible for child protection and mental health services, for example, to be based on notions of dignity and the inherent worth of persons. If they are not, what are the values that underpin them?

Conclusion

In June 2016, the UN's Committee on Economic, Social and Cultural Rights published a damning report that stated that the impact of the governments's policies of austerity and welfare reform amount to a breach of their obligations under human rights policies. In particular, they highlighted: the fact that more people were reliant on food banks; high rates of unemployment; the poor provision of mental health care; an increase in homelessness and; increasing discrimination against migrants. The UN Committee highlighted the disproportionate adverse impact that austerity measures has on the most disadvantaged and marginalised individuals and groups. The report concluded that the UK government policy of austerity had a disproportionate impact on the most vulnerable (United Nations Economic and Social Council, 2016).

Borrowing the phrase from Gramsci, Wacquant outlines the development of a 'centaur state'. In this new model, the state has retreated from a number of areas, most notably regulation of the market. However, for the urban poor, the state's scope and extent of state regulation has increased, with the expansion of the use of imprisonment being the clearest demonstration of this phenomenon. Social work has increasingly been drawn into these processes. Wacquant's work provides a stark contrast to those who see class as an analytical tool that is no longer valid. As Garrett (2013) notes in Giddens' (1998) *The Third Way*, which established his credentials as New Labour's intellectual guru, class seems to have been replaced by a series of lifestyle choices that appear to have been increased by financial capitalism. In this process, Fraser (2013a) argues that representation rather than redistribution has become the focus of social movements.

Social work as a profession often struggles to define its role or underpinning professional values and to engage with wider social theory. When Jacqui Smith introduced changes to social work training in 2002, she made it clear that she saw social work as essentially a practical task. In this framework, service users (possibly not the term that would be used in this model) want and require assistance, not an ideologically driven analysis of their situation. This caricature of the social worker obsessed with political correctness at the expense of the needs of those they are working with could have come straight from the pages of the *Daily Mail*. Like many in the profession, I experienced a mild state of shock from hearing the Prime Minister's tribute to "noble" social workers at the Conservative Party conference (Fraser, 2013b). The new Frontline (see www.thefrontline.org.uk/our-programme)

scheme to recruit graduates to children and families' social work has many weaknesses. However, it does, at least, explicitly acknowledge that social workers need to be critical thinkers. The exercise of professional judgement can only be taken from a strong and theoretical value base.

Taylor (2003) argues that common sense or more widely held views are often not outlined in theoretical or abstract form. The importance of images, stories and popular myths should not be underestimated. This has particular resonance in the area of social and welfare policy. The tabloid media, alongside populist TV documentaries, have had a pivotal role in framing a discourse that welfare is a state subsidy for 'feckless scroungers'. As Welshman's (2013) analysis demonstrates, this discourse has been in existence for over 200 years, and seems to be recast in a new form every 20 or 30 years. However, it appears particularly virulent in its current iteration. This is an important issue for social work. As a profession, it is committed to social justice so should therefore challenge this discrimination and classism. In addition, these attitudes are actually at the root of many policy developments that have seen the marginalisation of social work based on relational ideas. A possible way forward is to combine the sociological insights of the work of scholars such as Wacquant with an ethical approach to the face-to-face encounter inspired by Levinas. The strength of Wacquant's work is the analysis of the structural, economic and spatial inequalities that social workers need to challenge if they are to practice in a way that is consistent with the IFSW (2014) definition of the profession. Social work needs to reinvigorate a professional culture that sees the poor, marginalised and excluded not as sites of risk, but as fellow citizens. An ethical approach inspired by Levinas would require social work to put aside the professional processes of Othering in which it has become embroiled.

Conclusion

In this concluding chapter I summarise the key themes of the book, and make some suggestions about how social work can reassert its core mission and commitment to social justice. I have argued here that neoliberalism has to be understood as a political and economic project. There are a number of key elements within it. Neoliberalism as a political philosophy is based on a belief that unfettered markets are the most effective mechanism for the distribution of resources. It is claimed by neoliberalism's most vocal supporters that markets are 'natural', and any attempt to interfere with them is doomed to failure. The market is presented as an unfettered mechanism of exchange between rational individuals. As Hall (2011) and Harcourt (2011) note, this is actually a somewhat idealised notion. However, the doxa of free market economics have become deeply entrenched within political and public policy discourse. Progressive parties have shifted Right-wards in their stance in the belief that they would not win elections on a traditional programme of commitment to investment in public services funded through direct taxation. The Blair and Clinton administrations followed this path so that they would not be outflanked on this issue.

Neoliberalism is a social as well as economic phenomenon. Its economic beliefs and views on a range of social issues are intertwined and cannot be divorced one from the other. Neoliberals have a view of the world that sees it as a competitive environment. Markets reward success and punish failure. Individuals succeed because of their own hard work, effort, skills and entrepreneurial vim. From this perspective, refusal to acknowledge this is either naive or the first steps to the establishment of 'big government'. From this set of beliefs springs mistrust in the social state. Any moves for the state or government agencies to increase their powers or jurisdiction should be resisted at all costs. Government bureaucracies are, in this schema, not subject to the disciplines of the market such as the laws of supply and demand or competition. This means that they are naturally inefficient. The role of the state is to ensure that free markets can operate, ensure the safety of the citizen and defend the realm. The modern state that has taken a role in education, healthcare and transport, among many other areas, needs to be significantly reduced.

It is perhaps not that surprising that neoliberals' anti-statism is most apparent in attitudes to the welfare state – or, more accurately, payments made to those who are out of work. The first objection is that such benefits are too generous. They therefore allow individuals to opt out of the rigours of employment for a lifestyle that is subsidised by the taxpayer. This dependency is seen as a moral issue because it undermines the self-reliance of the individual. The welfare state is also seen as rewarding individuals for anti-social behaviour or protecting people from the consequences of poor choices. In addition, because the state provides for children, it is argued that this allows men to walk away from their parental responsibilities. The final argument against the welfare state is that it costs too much and that it is paid for out of taxation. The burden of that taxation falls on the middle and upper classes who are least likely to use these services. These trends came together under the umbrella of 'austerity', which has to be understood as a continuance of a clear neoliberal agenda to reduce the size of the welfare state.

The cumulative effect of austerity policies can be seen in the underfunding of public services and the reduction in income of the poorest members of society. As the acerbic Blyth (2013b) reminds us, the whole policy is based on the fundamental premise that the poorest members of society have to pay for the errors of some of the wealthiest. Public debt has also increased, so austerity fails on its own internal logic. At this point, it is worth reiterating the impact of some of the changes that have been introduced. The abolition of the Educational Maintenance Allowance (EMA) and the trebling of tuition fees are part of the shift in the generational dynamic of poverty. BASW UK calculates that changes to welfare and tax credits mean that there will be a further 266,000 children living in poverty by 2020. In the period 2010-16, local authorities faced a 30 per cent reduction in their budgets, and by 2020, early intervention funding for young people and families will have fallen by 71 per cent. Adult social care faces a crisis. This is often portrayed as being solely the result of demographic pressures, and ignores or minimises cuts to the funding of adult social care and the impact of the underfunding of the NHS.

Beckett and Western (2001) argue that wider social policy is inextricably linked with developments in penal policy. In their analysis, political cultures that emphasise social causes of marginality and offending are much more likely to have a penal policy based on integration. The result will be lower rates of imprisonment. At the other end of this continuum, cultures that conceptualise social problems largely as the result of individual failings will lead to harsher views on crime and thus higher rates of imprisonment. The welfare and penal systems cannot be divorced from each other. Both have become more punitive. The expansion of the penal state has slowed, but there are still plans to build a series of mega prisons.

Policies reflect wider social and cultural attitudes. I have argued that these have become generally harsher. For example, the Legal Aid, Sentencing and Punishment of Offenders Act (LASPO) 2012 led to significant restrictions on the availability of legal aid. It was no longer available in cases involving, for example, debt, education and housing. Amnesty International (2016) subsequently reported that there were 2,500 fewer legal aid cases in the field of immigration involving children. In the first year of LASPO there was a fall of 46 per cent in the number of cases, 925,000 in 2012–13 down to just 497,000. In social welfare law, the number of cases was down by 99 per cent. These changes have the effect of creating or further entrenching a two-tier legal system.

In April 2017, changes were introduced to the child tax credit system with the roll out of Universal Credit. As part of these moves the 'child element' of Universal Credit was limited to two children. However, if a mother can show a third child was 'conceived as a result of non-consensual sex' or that the third or subsequent child was 'conceived in a controlling and coercive relationship', she would be able to claim. If the woman was still living with the partner, the payment would not be made. If we stop and think for a moment, this means that the Universal Credit system will only support a third child if the mother can demonstrate that she was the victim of sexual violence.

Levitas (2012) notes that the response to the 2011 riots included calls for the families of those convicted of offences to be evicted from social housing. The Courts also sentenced those convicted during the disturbances to much longer terms of imprisonment than would be normal for shoplifting, criminal damage and similar offences. Taken alongside measures such as the 'Bedroom Tax' and changes to Housing Benefit for young people, these policies enforce the view that welfare policy has increasingly become a series of naked disciplinary measures.

As society has become more unequal over the past 30 years, there has been a shift in attitudes towards the poor. The work of Tyler (2008), Jensen and Tyler (2015) and others demonstrates the ways in which tabloid media and reality TV programmes have helped shape an anti-welfare, anti-poor discourse. The key themes of this discourse are that the welfare state is bloated and creates dependency, benefits are too generous, all those living on benefits are defrauding the system in some way and that the country can no longer afford the welfare state. To these anti-welfare state main themes we could add the idea that the system encourages the poor to have too many children and that it is exploited by immigrants. The advent of reality TV and poverty porn has also created an environment where those struggling in poverty can be paraded before the rest of society for their entertainment and derision.

Alongside this ideological attack on the whole basis of the social contract and the post-war welfare settlement has been an increase in the so-called 'marketisation' of the state. This can be seen most prominently in the area of social care. For example, Virgin Care recently won a £9 million contract to run adult social care for a council in the west of England. The seven-year deal will see the company take over three important areas of council provision: adult social care, community healthcare and continuing healthcare provided to those leaving hospital, which is funded by the NHS. Such plans have not yet been introduced into children and families' social work.

The government has, however, been much more supportive of charities and the third sector. For example, Kids Company, before its ignominious decline and eventual collapse, was presented as the epitome of the model organisation of the type that Cameron saw as the basis of his 'Big Society'. It was seen as providing (and certainly presented itself as providing) a radical child-centred alternative to the staid bureaucracy of local authority social work. It was founded in 1996 by Camila Batmanghelidjh, who became a prominent public figure who appeared to have the ear of both the Blair and Cameron governments. The Select Affairs Committee's inquiry into the collapse of Kids Company notes that despite concerns being raised about the organisation, successive governments provided Kids Company with grants of at least £42 million. This is in addition to the celebrity support and donations that the organisation was able to receive. For example, the band Coldplay donated millions of pounds to support various projects. It is difficult to imagine that governments or rock stars would have supported a public sector organisation in such a fashion.

Neoliberal policies followed by a period of austerity – a more potent form of the same brew – has created a much more divided and unequal society. As well as economic inequality, there has been a fairly constant demonising of the poor, vulnerable and marginalised. This is the logic of a view that sees society as made of winners and losers – praising winners and denigrating losers. These trends have been exacerbated by social and mainstream media's employment of a series of 'commentators' following the US cable network model of Right-wing shock jocks – Clarkson, Littlejohn and Liddle – to produce weekly attacks on the liberal elite (they are, of course, not part of any elite), and to denigrate the poor, minority ethnic groups, asylum-seekers and refugees. This reached a new low when, in April 2015, Katie Hopkins wrote a column for *The Sun* – the biggest selling daily newspaper – which was headlined 'Rescue boats? I'd use gunships to stop migrants.' The comment piece included the following:

> NO, I don't care. Show me pictures of coffins, show me bodies floating in water, play violins and show me skinny people looking sad. I still don't care.

and:

> Make no mistake, these migrants are like cockroaches. They might look a bit "Bob Geldof's Ethiopia circa 1984", but they are built to survive a nuclear bomb. They are survivors.

It is not that I am shocked by Hopkins' racist bile, but the fact that it could be published in a national newspaper should be astonishing.

Social work has responded to the humanitarian crisis in line with its commitment to social justice. For example, Shareen Denman, a social work student at the University of Salford, established Salford to Calais. She raised funds, transport and donations, and travelled to Calais (see www.salford.ac.uk/students/news/salford-to-calais). This project was supported by students across the university, demonstrating that progressive values have a potentially ongoing appeal for students – from all disciplines, not just social work.

Social work and social work values have found themselves in a cold, sometimes freezing, climate for a prolonged period. The question is, how does a profession such as social work, committed to social justice, counter these trends? There are two elements to this. The first is that on a national and international scale, social work as a profession has a commitment to progressive values and campaigns for social justice. In April 2017 BASW UK members marched from their HQ in Birmingham to their national conference in Liverpool under the banner 'Boot Out Austerity', to highlight the impact of cuts in social work provision and also the effect on tax and welfare changes. IFSW's Global Agenda seeks to:

- Promote social and economic equalities
- Promote the dignity and worth of peoples
- Work towards environmental and community sustainability
- Strengthen recognition of the importance of human relationships

On another level, on a daily basis individual social workers work alongside service users, often in increasingly difficult environments, to challenge these notions that degrade and denigrate fellow citizens. At the basis of these relationships is a fundamental recognition of humanity and dignity. In my work, students and practitioners have generally not lost their commitment to working towards social justice. Despite the best efforts of successive governments and policy changes, social workers do not want to become bureaucratic functionaries. One of the reasons that the Munro review was so welcomed in social work was that it focused on the autonomy and professional decision-making of practitioners.

Trends may be towards a more bureaucratic and procedural form of social work practice, but within that there is, and always has been, scope for individual workers to challenge or quietly subvert – something that social workers tend to be very skilled at and relish (White, 2009; Carey and Foster, 2011). Lipsky (1980) argues that power is exercised by 'street level bureaucrats', and that social workers, alongside other professions such as the police, form a 'policy-making community'. White (2009) argues that since the 1980s, changes in the profession have created an atmosphere where many social workers feel disillusioned and under siege. Warner (2015) demonstrates that these feelings have intensified following the political exploitation of the death of 'Baby P'. Social workers have not simply passively accepted this managerialist shift. White (2009) identifies two responses that she terms 'resistance through distance' and 'resistance through persistence'. The first describes the ways in which social workers can carve out a creative space in which to practice. The second captures the ways in which social workers can use their expertise to challenge decision-making and hold managers to account as a means of advocating on behalf of service users.

Social work and its poverty paradox

Social work takes place within a specific political and cultural context. The current one is where poverty and inequality are increasing. Backwith (2015) suggests that alongside this increase in inequality, state welfare systems have become more punitive. Access to state support in all forms is becoming more and more restrictive. In this environment, the scope for statutory social work to address these issues is more limited. For example, Backwith (2015) points out that the destitution of asylum-seekers is not some unfortunate by-product of government policy; it *is* government policy. In these areas, social work in particular fields has increasingly moved to the voluntary or non-statutory sector where there is, perhaps, more scope to work in an individualised or non-procedural manner.

Mantle and Backwith (2010) identify three broad approaches and responses to the issues of poverty. A critical or radical social work perspective sees the causes of poverty as lying in capitalism, while a systems approach seeks to link individuals to community resources and networks. The final approach that can be termed a bureaucratic or functionalist one focuses on individuals or families. Bureaucratic approaches have become more dominant in recent times. A shift would lead to a model that sees social workers playing a role in developing community resources and assets – 'social capital', in Bourdieu's terms – such as credit unions, social clubs, activities for young people – while at the same time campaigning on broader social policy issues such as cuts to welfare benefits for people living with disabilities. Alongside this community development role social workers can work alongside individuals living in poverty to mitigate these issues. Monnickendam et al (2010) emphasise that these issues are one of the fundamental dilemmas in social work practice. The profession's self-proclaimed grand mission of social change is actually achieved in individuals' lives. Thus, change takes place on a micro level. Social work clearly plays a role on a macro level in the way that the profession's leaders influence or attempt to shape government policy. However, these realms are far removed from social workers facing the challenges of working with increasingly limited resources.

The work of Mantle and Backwith (2010), Backwith (2015) and Krumer-Nevo (2015) highlights what I term the 'poverty paradox' in social work education and practice experience. I outline this as follows. Social work as a profession commits itself to social justice and therefore to tackling poverty and inequality. Significant numbers of service users are living in or at risk of poverty. However, social workers' awareness of the impact of poverty appears to be low. This creates a tendency to view the causes of poverty as individual rather than structural – an approach that has more in common with neoliberalism and is at odds with the expressed value base of the profession. The result is a shift in focus to psychodynamic theoretical approaches. In addition, the impact of poverty on communities and individuals is presented in a pathologised form. In the area of child protection, they are concerns that poverty – driven by austerity – has been recast as an issue of parental neglect. Poverty forms a backdrop to much social work practice, but is curiously absent from many discussions about the nature of that work. There are some notable exceptions to this – the work of Bywaters (2015a, 2015b) and Bywaters et al (2014a, 2014b) in this country is an excellent example. The work of the Re-Imagining Social Work (RSW) NZ collective (see www.reimaginingsocialwork.nz) is another radical attempt to shift the focus so that families experiencing poverty are not facing the double jeopardy of state intervention on the basis that low income means that they are not meeting societal parenting norms.

One of the aims of this book is to support the work of my colleagues who have refused to allow debates about the nature and impact of class, poverty and inequality to be removed from broader discussions about the role of social work. I would argue that one of the impacts of neoliberalism has been for a focus on poverty and inequality to be marginalised. An irony of the banking crisis and its aftermath, including the introduction of policies based on austerity, is that they have reignited interest in these issues. There is an increasingly diverse literature that examines these issues in contemporary Britain. This work includes analyses of the roots of the crash and the imposition of austerity (Blyth, 2013b; Sayer, 2015) as well as work that examines the lived experiences of those who have been most affected by cuts in public service provision introduced by the coalition government (Lansley and Mack, 2015; O'Hara, 2015; Garthwaite, 2016a). Social work and social workers are often marginal in these accounts of individuals, families and communities who are responding to the challenges of daily living in these circumstances. This is in contrast to other works, where those living in poverty are portrayed as helpless and the hapless victims of broader social forces.

Krumer-Nevo (2015) outlines what she terms a 'poverty aware paradigm' that would inform a new attempt for social work to engage with tackling poverty. She suggests that this would require social work education and training to place poverty more centrally in the curricula. She argues that an analysis of poverty has to start from the proposition that poverty is a violation of human rights. As noted above, in recent times these broader considerations of social work have been marginalised. Social justice approaches to poverty and social work would require that students engage with the various theoretical approaches to these issues. For example, Pierce (1970) outlined what he termed 'microaggressions' that African Americans were and are still daily subject to in racist society. A similar approach can be used to examine the experiences of those living in poverty. Social work students and practitioners need to examine what role they play in these processes, and how they might change professional attitudes and behaviours. The messages from service users are often that their experience of social work processes is not positive. Social work, despite its professional value statements, is not immune from negative attitudes.

Throughout this book I have attempted to highlight that social work continues to suffer from what Gill and Jack (2007) term 'poverty blindness'. Experiences of poverty are such a key and regular feature of service users' lived experience that they become marginalised in their engagement with services. This is the root of the poverty paradox. This is not to suggest that individual social workers are not committed to tackling poverty and social exclusion. This clearly remains the case. Fortunately, despite the rise and rise of managerialism, social workers remain committed to the key principles of social justice. The challenge is to create and sustain a professional working environment that does not see these values ground into dust by the bureaucratic cultures that remove the scope for autonomy and the exercise of professional judgement (Munro, 2011). Alongside these approaches, I have argued that there is a requirement for the constant restatement of social work's core values and moral principles. This can be done on an individual, organisational and professional level.

If social work is not a critical voice based on progressive and humane values, it is nothing.

References

1990 Trust (2010) *The price of race inequality: the black manifesto 2010,* 1990 Trust (www.diversecymru.org.uk/wp-content/uploads/The-Black-Manifesto-2010.pdf).

Academy of Medical Royal Colleges and Royal College of Psychiatrists (2009) *No health without mental health: The supporting evidence,* London: Academy of Medical Royal Colleges and Royal College of Psychiatrists.

Adams, T. (2013) 'Jazz fan, hipster and a leftwing hero: The remarkable journey of Stuart Hall', *The Guardian,* 18 August (www.theguardian.com/society/2013/aug/18/professor-stuart-hall-multiculturalism-film).

Alexander, M. (2012) *The new Jim Crow: Mass incarceration in the age of colorblindness,* New York, NY: New Press.

Allen, R., Ashworth, A., Cotterrell, R., Coyle, A., Duff, A., Lacey, N., Liebling, A. and Morgan, R. (2014) *A presumption against imprisonment: Social order and social values,* London: British Academy (www.britac.ac.uk/policy/Presumption_Against_Imprisonment.cfm).

Amnesty International (2016) *Cuts that hurt: The impact of legal aid cuts in England on access to justice,* London: Amnesty International (www.amnesty.org/en/documents/eur45/4936/2016/en/).

Annison, J. (2007) 'A gendered review of change within the probation service', *The Howard Journal of Crime and Justice,* vol 46, no 2, pp 145-61.

Appiah, K. (2007) *Cosmopolitanism: Ethics in a world of strangers,* London: Penguin.

Arendt, H. (1963) *Eichmann in Jerusalem: A report on the banality of evil,* New York, NY: Penguin.

Backwith, D. (2015) *Social work, poverty and social exclusion,* Maidenhead: Open University Press.

Badiou, A. (2015) *Theoretical writings* (Bloomsbury Revelations), London: Bloomsbury.

Bakhtin, M.M. (1984) *Rabelais and his world (vol 341),* Bloomington, IN: Indiana University Press.

Barker, V. (2012) 'Global mobility and penal order: criminalizing migration, a view from Europe', *Sociology Compass,* vol 6, no 2, pp 113-21.

Barnes, M. (2006) *Caring and social justice,* Basingstoke: Palgrave.

Barr, B., Taylor-Robinson, D., Stuckler, D., Loopstra, R., Reeves, A. and Whitehead, M. (2015) '"First do no harm": Are disability assessments associated with adverse trends in mental health? A longitudinal study', *Journal of Epidemiology & Community Health*.

Barstow, S. (2013) *A kind of loving* (50th edn), Swansea: Parthian [originally published in 1960].

Barton, W.R. (1959) *Institutional neurosis*, Bristol: Wright & Sons.

BASW (British Association of Social Workers) (no date) 'Understanding the PCF' (www.basw.co.uk/pcf/understanding-the-pcf/).

Bauman, Z. (2000) 'Special essay. Am I my brother's keeper?', *European Journal of Social Work*, vol 3, no 1, pp 5-11.

Bauman, Z. (1989) *Modernity and the Holocaust*, Ithaca, NY: Cornell University Press.

Bauman, Z. (2008) *The art of life*, Cambridge: Polity Press.

Beck, U. (1992) *Risk society: Towards a new modernity*, London: Sage.

Beck, U. (1999) *What is globalization?*, Cambridge: Polity Press.

Beck, U. (2008) *World at risk*, Cambridge: Polity Press.

Becker, G.S. (1968) 'Crime and punishment: An economic approach', *Journal of Political Economy*, vol 76, pp 169-217.

Beckett, K. and Western, B. (2001) 'Governing social marginality', in D. Garland (ed) *Mass imprisonment: Social causes and consequences*, London: Sage, pp 35-50.

Beddoe, L. (2014) 'Feral families, troubled families: The spectre of the underclass in New Zealand', *NZ Sociology*, vol 29, no 3, pp 51-68.

Berger, P. (1970) 'On the obsolescence of the concept of honor', *European Journal of Sociology*, pp 339-47.

Berman, G. (2012) *Prison population statistics*, London: House of Commons Library.

Bew, J. (2016) *Citizen Clem: A biography of Attlee*, London: Riverrun.

Bilson, A. and Martin, K.E. (2016) 'Referrals and child protection in England: One in five children referred to children's services and one in nineteen investigated before the age of five', *The British Journal of Social Work*, p.bcw.054.

Blyth, M. (2013a) 'Why a bad idea won over the West', *Foreign Affairs*, June (www.foreignaffairs.com/articles/139105/mark-blyth/the-austerity-delusion).

Blyth, M. (2013b) *Austerity: History of a dangerous idea*, Oxford: Oxford University Press.

Boltanski, L. and Chiapello, E. (2005) 'The new spirit of capitalism', *International Journal of Politics, Culture, and Society*, vol 18, no 3-4, pp 161-88.

Booth, W. (1890) *In darkest England and the way out*, London: International Headquarters of the Salvation Army.

Booth, C. (1903) *Life and labour of the people in London (volume 8)*, London: Macmillan and Company.

Borrie, S.G, (1994) *Report of the Commission on Social Justice*, London: Institute for Public Policy Research (www.ippr.org/publications/social-justice-strategies-for-national-renewal).

Bourdieu, P. (1998) 'The left hand and the right hand of the state', in P. Bourdieu (ed) *Acts of resistance*, pp 1-10.

Bourdieu, P. (2005) *The social structures of the economy*, Cambridge: Polity.

Bourdieu, P. (2010) *Distinction* (Routledge Classics), London: Routledge.

Bourdieu, P. and Wacquant, L. (1992) *An invitation to reflexive sociology*, Chicago, IL: University of Chicago Press.

Bourdieu, P. et al (1999) *The weight of the world: Social suffering in contemporary society: Social suffering and impoverishment in contemporary society*, Cambridge: Polity Press.

Bowcott, O. and Butler, P. (2016) 'Families win supreme court appeals over "unfair" bedroom tax', *The Guardian*, 9 November (www.theguardian.com/society/2016/nov/09/families-win-supreme-court-appeals-over-unfair-bedroom-tax-jacqueline-carmichael).

Bradshaw, J. (ed) (2011) *The well-being of children in the UK* (4th edn), Bristol: Policy Press.

Brady, D. (2009) *Rich democracies, poor people: How politics explain poverty*, Oxford: Oxford University Press.

Braine, J. (1957) *Room at the top*, London: Arrow Books.

Brandt, A.M. (1978) 'Racism and research: the case of the Tuskegee Syphilis Study', *Hastings Center Report*, vol 8, no 6, pp 21-29.

Bronfenbrenner, U. (1979) *The ecology of human development: Experiments by nature and design*, Cambridge, MA: Harvard University Press.

Bunting, M. (2011) 'Can the spread of women's rights ever be accompanied by war?', *The Guardian*, 2 October (www.theguardian.com/commentisfree/2011/oct/02/women-rights-afghanistan-war-west).

Butler, I. and Drakeford, M. (2001) 'Which Blair project? Communitarianism, social authoritarianism and social work', *Journal of Social Work*, vol 1, pp 7-19.

Butler, J. (2004) *Precarious life: The powers of mourning and violence*, London: Verso.

Bywaters, P. (2015a) 'Inequalities in child welfare: Towards a new policy, research and action agenda', *British Journal of Social Work*, vol 45, no 1, pp 6-23.

Bywaters, P. (2015b) 'Cumulative jeopardy? A response to Brown and Ward', *Children and Youth Services Review*, vol 52, pp 68-73 (http://dx.doi.org/10.1016/j.childyouth.2015.03.001).

Bywaters, P., Brady, G., Sparks, T. and Bos, E. (2014a) 'Child welfare inequalities: New evidence, further questions', *Child & Family Social Work* (http://dx.doi.org/10.1111/cfs.12154).

Bywaters, P., Brady, G., Sparks, T. and Bos, E. (2014b) 'Inequalities in child welfare intervention rates: The intersection of deprivation and identity', *Child & Family Social Work* (http://dx.doi.org/10.1111/cfs.12161).

Bywaters, P., Bunting, L., Davidson, G., Hanratty, J., Mason, W., McCartan, C. and Steils, N. (2016) *The relationship between poverty, child abuse and neglect: An evidence review*, London: Joseph Rowntree Foundation.

Cameron, D. (2010) 'Prime Minister's speech on the economy, Milton Keynes', 7 June (www.gov.uk/government/speeches/prime-ministers-speech-on-the-economy).

Campbell, J. and Davidson, G. (2012) *Post-qualifying mental health social work practice*, London: Sage.

Carey, J. (2012) *The Intellectuals and the masses: Pride and prejudice among the literary intelligentsia 1880-1939*, London: Faber & Faber.

Carey, M. and Foster, V. (2011) 'Introducing "deviant" social work: Contextualising the limits of radical social work whilst understanding (fragmented) resistance within the social work labour process', *British Journal of Social Work*, vol 41, no 3, pp 576-93.

Carson, E. and Golinelli, D. (2013) 'Prisoners in 2012: Trends in admissions and releases 1991-2013' (www.bjs.gov/content/pub/pdf/p12tar9112.pdf).

Casey, L. (2016) 'Lessons from Rotherham and my work with troubled families', in E. Solomon (ed) *Rethinking children's services: Fit for the future?* (www.catch-22.org.uk/collaborate/current-collaboration/rethinking-childrens-services/).

Caspi, A., Houts, R.M., Belsky, D.W., Harrington, H., Hogan, S., Ramrakha, S. et al (2016) 'Childhood forecasting of a small segment of the population with large economic burden', *Nature*.

Cavadino, M. and Dignan, J. (with others) (2006) *Penal systems: A comparative approach*, London: Sage Publications.

Cavadino, M., Crow, I. and Dignan, J. (1999) *Criminal justice 2000*, Reading: Waterside Press.

Centre for Welfare Reform (2015) *A fair society?*, Sheffield: Centre for Welfare Reform (www.centreforwelfarereform.org).

Chang, H. (2011) 23 *things they don't tell you about capitalism*, London: Pelican.

Chang, H. (2014) *Economics: The user's guide*, London: Pelican.

Chase, E. and Walker, R. (2013) 'The co-construction of shame in the context of poverty: Beyond a threat to the social bond', *Sociology*, vol 47, no 4, pp 739-54.

Cheshire, J. and O'Brien, O. (2012) 'Lives on the line: Life expectancy and child poverty as a tube map' (http://spatialanalysis.co.uk/2012/07/lives-on-the-line/).

Children's Society, The (2012) 'UK asylum system forces thousands of children to live in severe poverty', Press release, 9 April (www.childrenssociety.org.uk/news-and-blogs/press-release/uk-asylum-system-forces-thousands-children-live-severe-poverty).

Clear, T. (2009) *Imprisoning communities: How mass incarceration makes disadvantaged neighborhoods worse*, New York: Oxford University Press.

Cohen, S. (2006) *Deportation is freedom: The Orwellian world of immigration controls*, London: Jessica Kingsley Publishers.

Cohen, S. (2011) *Folk devils and moral panics* (Routledge Classics), Oxford: Routledge.

Conservative Party (2008) *Control shift returning power to local communities: Responsibility agenda policy green paper no.9*, Conservative Party (www.isitfair.co.uk/Downloads/Returning_Power_Local_Communities.pdf).

Corston, J. (Chair) (2008) *Review of women with particular vulnerabilities in the criminal justice system*, London: HMSO.

Crawford, R. (2010) 'Public services: serious cuts to come', Emergency Budget June 2010 briefing, London: Institute for Fiscal Studies (www.ifs.org.uk/budgets/budgetjune2010/crawford.pdf).

Cross, S. (2010) *Mediating madness: Mental distress and cultural representation*, Basingstoke: Palgrave Macmillan.

Crossley, S. (2015a) 'Realising the (troubled) family: Crafting the neoliberal state', *Families, Relationships and Societies*, vol 5, no 2, pp 263-79.

Crossley, S.J. (2015b) *The troubled families programme: The perfect social policy?* London: Centre for Crime and Justice Studies.

C-Span (1996) 'Mrs Clinton campaign speech', 25 January 1996, Keene State University, NH, (www.c-span.org/video/?69606-1/mrs-clinton-campaign-speech).

Cummins, I.D. (2011) 'Distant voices, still lives: Reflections on the impact of the media reporting of the cases of Christopher Clunis and Ben Silcock', *Ethnicity and Inequalities in Health and Social Care,* vol 3, no 4, pp 18-29.

Cummins, I.D. (2012) 'Using Simon's Governing through crime to explore the development of mental health policy in England and Wales since 1983', *Journal of Social Welfare and Family Law*, vol 34, no 3, pp 325-37.

Cummins, I.D. (2013) '*The Sun* splash missed point on "mental patient murders"', *The Conversation*, 8 October (https://theconversation.com/the-sun-splash-missed-point-on-mental-patient-murders-18971).

Cummins, I.D. (2014) 'Time after time: a review of John Akomfrah's The Stuart Hall project: revolution, politics and the new experience', *European Group for the Study of Deviance and Social Control: Newsletter* (http://usir.salford.ac.uk/35486/).

Cummins, I.D. (2015) 'Discussing race, racism and mental health: Two mental health inquiries reconsidered', *International Journal of Human Rights in Healthcare*, vol 8, no 3, pp 160-72.

Cummins, I.D. and Edmondson, D. (2015) 'Policing and street triage', *Journal of Adult Protection*, vol 18, issue 1, pp 40-52.

Dallek, R. (2004) *Lyndon B. Johnson: Portrait of a president*, London: Penguin.

Dangerfield, A. (2012) 'Tube map used to plot Londoners' life expectancy', BBC, 20 July (www.bbc.co.uk/news/uk-england-london-18917932).

Department for Education (DfE) (2015) 'Characteristics of children in need: 2014 to 2015', London: DfE (www.gov.uk/government/uploads/system/uploads/attachment_data/file/469737/SFR41-2015_Text.pdf).

Distelberg, B. and Taylor, S. (2013) 'The roles of social support and family resilience in accessing healthcare and employment resources among families living in traditional public housing communities', *Child and Family Social Work*.

Donzelot, J. (1979) *The policing of families*, Baltimore, MD: Johns Hopkins University.

Dorling, D. (2015) *Inequality and the 1%*, London: Verso.

Dorling, D., Rigby, J., Wheeler, B., Ballas, D., Thomas, B., Fahmy, E. et al (2007) *Poverty, wealth and place in Britain, 1968 to 2005*, Bristol: Policy Press.

Downes, D. and Hansen, K. (2006) *Welfare and punishment. The relationship between welfare spending and imprisonment*, London: Centre for Crime and Justice Studies (www.crimeandsociety.org.uk).

Drake, C. and Cayton, H. (1993) *Black metropolis: A study of Negro life in a northern city*, Chicago, IL: University of Chicago Press.

Drucker, E. (2011) *A plagues of prisons: The epidemiology of mass incarceration in America*, New York: New Press.

Drug Policy Alliance (2011) *Drug Policy Alliance and Global Commission on Drug Policy*, New York: Drug Policy Alliance (www.drugpolicy. org).

Dworkin, R. (1995) *Life's dominion*, London: HarperCollins.

Edwards, A. (1943) *Comparative occupation statistics for the United States 1870-1940* (www.census.gov/people/io/files/Cover%20page%20 ch1%20ch2%20ch3%20Occ%201870%20to%201940.pdf).

Ehrenreich, B. (1990) *The worst years of our lives: Irreverent notes from a decade of greed*, New York: Pantheon Books.

Elias, N. and Scotson, J. (1994) *The established and the outsiders: A sociological enquiry into community problems*, London: Sage.

Emejulu, A. (2008) 'The intersection of ethnicity, poverty and wealth', in T. Ridge and S. Wright (eds) *Understanding inequality, poverty and wealth*, Bristol: Policy Press, pp 155-80.

Emejulu, A. and Bassel, L. (2015) 'Minority women, austerity and activism', *Race & Class*, vol 57, no 2.

Esping-Andersen, G. (1990) *The three worlds of welfare capitalism*, Cambridge: Polity Press.

Esping-Andersen, G. (1996) *Welfare states in transition: National adaptations in global economies*, Cambridge: Polity Press.

Esping-Andersen, G. (2002) *Why we need a new welfare state*, New York: Oxford University Press.

Etzioni, A. (1993) *The spirit of community: Rights, responsibilities, and the communitarian agenda*, New York: Crown.

Featherstone, B., White, S. and Morris, K. (2014) *Re-imagining child protection: Towards humane social work with families*, Bristol: Policy Press.

Fell, B. and Fell, P. (2013) 'Welfare across borders: A social work process with adult asylum seekers', *British Journal of Social Work*, pp 1-18.

Fenton, J. (2014) 'Can social work education meet the neoliberal challenge head on?', *Critical and Radical Social Work*, vol 2, no 3, pp 321-55.

Fineman, M. (2004) *The autonomy myth a theory of dependency*, New York, NY: The New Press.

Fineman, M. (2008) 'The vulnerable subject: anchoring equality in the human condition', *Yale Journal of Law and Feminism*, vol 20, no 1, article 2.

Foot, J. (2015) *The man who closed the asylums: Franco Basaglia and the revolution in mental health care*, London: Verso.

Forrester, D., Goodman, K., Cocker, C., Binnie, C. and Jensch, G. (2009) 'What is the impact of public care on children's welfare? A review of research findings from England and Wales and their policy implications', *Journal of Social Policy*, vol 38, pp 439-56.

Foucault, M. (1977) *Discipline and punish: The birth of the prison* (translated by A. Sheridan), London: Penguin.

Foucault, M. (1982) 'The subject and power', *Critical Inquiry*, vol 8, no 4, pp 777-95.

Foucault, M. (2008) *The birth of biopolitics: Lectures at the Collège de France, 1978-1979* (translated by Graham Burchell), Basingstoke: Palgrave.

Fraser, N. (1995) 'From redistribution to recognition? Dilemmas of justice in a "post-socialist" age', *New Left Review*, vol 68.

Fraser, N. (1997) 'A rejoinder to Iris Young', *New Left Review*, vol 223, p 126.

Fraser, N. (2007) 'Feminist politics in the age of recognition: A two-dimensional approach to gender justice', *Studies in Social Justice,* vol 1, no 1, pp 23-35.

Fraser, N. (2009) 'Social justice in the age of identity politics', in G. Henderson and M. Waterstone (eds) *Geographic thought: A praxis perspective*, Abingdon: Routledge, pp 72-91.

Fraser, N. (2010) 'Who counts? Dilemmas of justice in a postWestphalian world', *Antipode*, vol 41, pp 281-97.

Fraser, N. (2013a) *The fortunes of feminism: From women's liberation to identity politics to anti-capitalism*, London: Verso.

Fraser, N. (2013b) 'How feminism became capitalism's handmaiden – and how to reclaim it', *The Guardian*, 14 October (www.theguardian.com/commentisfree/2013/oct/14/feminism-capitalist-handmaiden-neoliberal).

Friedman, M. (2002) *Capitalism and freedom* (49th anniversary edn), London: University of Chicago Press [originally published in 1962].

Fuller, S. (2011) *Humanity 2.0: What it means to be human past, present and future*, London: Palgrave Macmillan.

Galbraith., J.K. (1964) 'Economics and the quality of life', *Science*, vol 145, no 3628, pp 117-23.

Garland, D. (2001) *The culture of control: Crime and social order in contemporary society*, Oxford: Oxford University Press.

Garland, D. (2004) 'Beyond the culture of control', *Critical Review of International and Political Philosophy*, vol 7, no 2, pp 160-89.

Garland, D. (2014) 'What is the welfare state? A sociological restatement', London School of Economics and Political Science (www.lse.ac.uk/website-archive/newsAndMedia/videoAndAudio/channels/publicLecturesAndEvents/player.aspx?id=2695).

Garrett, P.M. (2002) 'Social work and the "just society": Diversity, difference and the sequestration of poverty', *Journal of Social Work*, vol 2, no 2, pp 187-210.

Garrett, P.M. (2007) 'Making social work more Bourdieusian: Why the social professions should critically engage with the work of Pierre Bourdieu', *European Journal of Social Work*, vol 10, no 2, pp 225-43.

Garrett, P.M. (2013) *Social work and social theory: Making connections*, Bristol: Policy Press.

Garrett, P.M. (2014) 'Re-enchanting social work? The emerging "spirit" of social work in an age of economic crisis', *British Journal of Social Work*, vol 44, no 3, pp 503-21.

Garrett, P.M. (2015) 'Confronting neoliberal penality: Placing prison reform and critical criminology at the core of social work's social justice agenda', *Journal of Social Work*, (http://journals.sagepub.com/doi/abs/10.1177/1468017314565753).

Garthwaite, K. (2016a) 'Stigma, shame and "people like us": An ethnographic study of food bank use in the UK', *Journal of Poverty and Social Justice*, vol 24, no 3, pp 277-89.

Garthwaite, K. (2016b) *Hunger pains: Life inside Foodbank Britain*, Bristol: Policy Press.

Gibney, M. (2004) *The ethics and politics of asylum*, Cambridge: Cambridge University Press.

Giddens, A. (1998) *The Third Way: The renewal of social democracy*, Oxford: Blackwell.

Gill, O. and Jack, G. (2007) *The child and family in context: Developing ecological practice in disadvantaged communities*, Lyme Regis: Russell House Publishing.

Gilligan, P. (2007) 'Well-motivated reformists or nascent radicals: How do applicants to the degree in social work see social problems, their origins and solutions?', *British Journal of Social Work*, vol 37, no 4, pp 735-60.

Gilmour, I. (1992) *Dancing with dogma: Britain under Thatcherism*, London: Simon & Schuster.

Gilroy, P. (2002) *There ain't no black in the Union Jack: The cultural politics of race and nation* (Routledge Classics), London: Routledge.

Giroux, H. (2011) 'Neoliberalism and the death of the social state: Remembering Walter Benjamin's Angel of History', *Social Identities: Journal for the Study of Race, Nation and Culture*, vol 17, issue 4.

Goffman, E. (1963) *Stigma: Notes on the management of spoiled identities*, New York: Simon & Schuster.

Goffman, E. (1974) *Frame analysis: An essay on the organization of experience*, Cambridge, MA: Harvard University Press.

Goldthorpe, J. (2010) *Affluent worker: Industrial attitudes and behaviour*, Cambridge: Cambridge University Press.

Gottschalk, M. (2006) *The prison and the gallows: The politics of mass incarceration in America*, Cambridge: Cambridge University Press.

Gough, I. (2000) *Global capital, human needs and social policies*, Basingstoke: Palgrave.

Gove, M. (2013) 'Michael Gove speech to the NSPCC: getting it right for children in need', 12 November (www.gov.uk/government/speeches/getting-it-right-for-children-in-need-speech-to-the-nspcc).

Gray, J.P. (2001) *Why our drug laws have failed and what can we do about it: A judicial indictment of the War on Drugs*, Philadelphia, PA: Temple University Press.

Green, D.A. (2008) *When children kill children: Penal populism and political culture*, Oxford: Oxford University Press.

Gupta, A. (2015) 'Poverty and shame–messages for social work', *Critical and Radical Social Work*, vol 3, no 1, pp 131-39.

Gupta, A., Featherstone, B. and White, S. (2014) 'Reclaiming humanity: from capacities to capabilities in understanding parenting in adversity', *The British Journal of Social Work*, vol 46, no 2, pp 339-54.

Habermas, J. (2010) 'The concept of human dignity and the realistic utopia of human rights', *Metaphilosophy*, vol 41, no 4, pp 468-80.

Hall, S. (1997) *Representation: Cultural representations and signifying practices*, London: Sage.

Hall, S. (2003) 'Creolization, diaspora, and hybridity in the context of globalization', in O. Enwezor, C. Basualdo, U.M. Bauer, S. Ghez, S. Maharaj, M. Nash and O. Zaya (eds) Documenta 11_Platform 3, pp 185-98.

Hall, S. (2011) 'The neo-liberal revolution', *Cultural studies*, vol 25, no 6, pp 705-28.

Hall, S. (2017a) *Familiar stranger: A life between two islands*, London: Penguin.

Hall, S. (2017b) 'The great moving right show', in S. Hall (ed) *Selected political writings, the great moving right show and other essays*, Durham, NC: Durham Duke University Press, pp 172-89.

Hall, S. (2017c) 'The great moving nowhere show', in S. Hall (ed) *Selected political writings, the great moving right show and other essays*, Durham, NC: Durham Duke University Press, pp 283-300.

Hall, S. and Jacques, M. (eds) (1983) *The politics of Thatcherism*, London: Lawrence and Wishart.

Hall, S., Critcher, C., Jefferson, T., Clarke, J. and Roberts, B. (2014) *Policing the crisis* (35th anniversary edn), Basingstoke: Palgrave.

Haney-Lopez, I. (2015) *Dog whistle politics: How coded racial appeals have reinvented racism and wrecked the middle class*, Oxford: Oxford University Press.

Hanley, L. (2012) *Estates: An intimate history*, London: Granta.

Hanley, L. (2016) *Respectable: The experience of class*, London: Penguin.

Hansen, T.B. and Stepputat, F. (2001) *States of imagination: Ethnographic explorations of the postcolonial state*, Durham, NC: Duke University Press.

Harcourt, B.E. (2011) *The illusion of free markets*, Cambridge, MA: Harvard University Press.

Hart, P. (2017) 'Disguised compliance – or undisguised nonsense?', *Family Law Week*, 10 April (www.familylawweek.co.uk/site.aspx?i=ed177164).

Harvey, D. (2005) *A brief history of neoliberalism*, Oxford: Oxford University Press.

Hayek, F. (2001) *The road to serfdom* (Routledge Classics), London: Routledge.

Hayes, D. and Spratt, T. (2014) 'Child welfare as child protection then and now: What social workers did and continue to do', *British Journal of Social Work*, vol 44, pp 615-35.

Herrnstein, R. and Murray, C. (1994) *The ell curve: Intelligence and class structure in American life*, New York: Simon & Schuster.

Hersh, S. (2004) 'Torture at Abu Ghraib', *The New Yorker*, 10 May (www.newyorker.com/magazine/2004/05/10/torture-at-abu-ghraib).

Hills, J. (2015) *Good times, bad times: The welfare myth of them and us*, Bristol: Policy Press.

Hinton, E. (2016) *From the War on Poverty to the War on Crime: The making of mass incarceration in America*, Cambridge, MA: Harvard University Press.

HMIP (HM Inspector of Prisons) (2013) *HM Chief Inspector of Prisons for England and Wales Annual Report 2012–13*, London: The Stationery Office.

Howard League for Penal Reform (2010) *Voice of a child*, London (www.howardleague.org).

Howe, D. (2014) *The complete social worker*, Basingstoke: Palgrave Macmillan.

Humphries, B. (2004a) 'An unacceptable role for social work: Implementing immigration policy', *British Journal of Social Work*, vol 34, pp 93-107.

Humphries, B. (2004b) 'Refugees, asylum-seekers, welfare and social work', in D. Hayes and B Humphries (eds) *Social work, immigration and asylum: Debates, dilemmas and ethical issues for social work and social care practice*, London: Jessica Kingsley Publisher, pp 42-58.

Hutton, W. (1995) *The state we're in*, London: Cape.

Hyslop, I.K. (2016) 'Where to social work in a brave new neoliberal Aotearoa?', *Aotearoa New Zealand Social Work*, vol 28, no 1, pp 5-12.

IFSW (International Federation of Social Workers) (2000) 'Definition of social work', (www.ifsw.org/ publications/4.6e.pub.html).

IFSW (2014) 'Global definition of social work', Berne: IFSW (http:// ifsw.org/policies/definition-of-social-work/).

Illich, I. (2003) 'Medical nemesis', *Journal of Epidemiology and Community Health*, vol 57, pp 919-22.

Institute for Fiscal Studies (2012) *Reforming council tax benefit*, IFS commentary 123 (www.ifs.org.uk/comms/comm123.pdf).

Jensen, T. (2013) 'Riots, restraint and the new cultural politics of wanting', *Sociological Research Online*, vol 18, no 4, p 7.

Jensen, T. and Tyler, I. (2015) '"Benefits broods": The cultural and political crafting of anti-welfare common sense', *Critical Social Policy*, vol 35, no 4, pp 1-22.

Jessop, B. (2002) 'Liberalism, neoliberalism, and urban governance: a state-theoretical perspective', *Antipode*, vol 34, no 3, pp 452-72.

Jones, C. and Novak, T. (1999) *Poverty, welfare and the disciplinary state*, London: Routledge.

Jones, O. (2011) *Chavs: The demonization of the working class*, London: Verso.

Jonson-Reid, M., Drake, B. and Kohl, P.L. (2009) 'Is the overrepresentation of the poor in child welfare caseloads due to bias or need?', *Children and Youth Services Review*, vol 31, no 3, pp 422-7.

Joseph Rowntree Foundation (JRF) (www.jrf.org.uk/report/uk-poverty-causes-costs-and-solutions).

Kant, I. (1996) *The metaphysics of morals* (Edited and translated by Mary J. Gregor), Cambridge: Cambridge University Press.

Kateb, G. (2011) *Human dignity*, Cambridge, MA: The Belknap Press.

Kelly, B. (2005) 'Structural violence and schizophrenia', *Social Science & Medicine*, vol 61, pp 721-30.

Knowles, C. (2000) *Bedlam on the streets*, Abingdon: Routledge.

Kohl, P.L., Johnson-Reid, M. and Drake, B. (2009) 'Time to leave substantiation behind: Findings from a national probability study', *Child Maltreatment*, vol 14, pp 17-26.

Krugman, P. (2015) 'The case for cuts was a lie. Why does Britain still believe it?', *The Guardian*, 29 April (www.theguardian.com/business/ng-interactive/2015/apr/29/the-austerity-delusion).

Krumer-Nevo, M. (2015) 'Poverty-aware social work: A paradigm for social work practice with people in poverty', *British Journal of Social Work*, vol 46, no 6, pp 1783-808.

Kynaston, D. (2007) *Austerity Britain, 1945-1951 (Tales of a New Jerusalem)*, London: Bloomsbury.

Kynaston, D. (2008) *Modernity Britain: 1957-1962*, London: Bloomsbury.

Lacey, N. (2008) *The prisoners' dilemma: Political economy and punishment in contemporary democracies*, Cambridge: Cambridge University Press.

Langan, M. (1998) *Welfare: Needs, rights and risks*, London: Routledge.

Lansley, S. and Mack, J. (2015) *Breadline Britain: The rise of mass poverty*, London: One World.

Leuchtenburg, W. (2009) *Franklin D. Roosevelt and the New Deal: 1932-1940*, London: HarperCollins.

Levinas, E. (1999) *Totality and infinity: An essay on exteriority*, Dordrecht: Kluwer Publishing.

Levinas, E. (2005) *Humanism of the other*, Dordrecht: Kluwer Publishing.

Levitas, R. (2012) *There may be 'trouble' ahead: What we know about those 120,000 'troubled' families*, Policy Response Series No 3, Poverty and Social Exclusion (www.poverty.ac.uk/policy-response-working-papers-families-social-policy-life-chances-children-parenting-uk-government).

Levy-Pounds, N. (2010) 'Can these bones live? A look at the impacts of the war on drugs on poor African-American children and families', *Hastings Race and Poverty Law Journal*, pp 353-80.

Lewis, O. (1969) *Five families: Mexican case studies in the culture of poverty*, New York: Basic Books.

Link, B. and Phelan, J. (2001) 'Conceptualizing stigma', *Annual Review of Sociology*, vol 27, pp 363-35.

Lipsky, M. (1980) *Street level bureaucracy: Dilemmas of the individual in public services*, New York: Russell Sage Foundation.

Lister, R. (1997) 'Citizenship: towards a feminist synthesis', *Feminist Review*, vol 57, no 1, pp 28-48.

Lister, R. (2004a) 'A politics of recognition and respect: involving people with experience of poverty in decision-making that affects their lives', in J. Andersen and B. Siim *The politics of inclusion and empowerment*, Basingstoke: Palgrave Macmillan, pp 116-38.

Lister, R. (2004b) *Poverty*, Cambridge: Polity Press.

Lister, R. (2015) '"To count for nothing": poverty beyond the statistics', *Journal of the British Academy*, vol 3, pp 139-65.

Littler, J. (2013) *Meritocracy as plutocracy: The marketising of 'equality' under neoliberalism*, Chadwell Heath: Lawrence & Wishart (www.lwbooks. co.uk/new-formations/80-81/meritocracy-plutocracy-marketising-equality-under-neoliberalism).

Littler, J. (2016) 'Mayritocracy: neoliberalism with new borders', Lawrence & Wishart blog, 22 November (www.lwbooks.co.uk/blog/mayritocracy-neoliberalism-with-new-borders).

Lockyer, S. (2010) 'Dynamics of social class contempt in contemporary British television comedy', *Social Semiotics*, vol 20, issue 2, pp 121-38.

Loopstra, R., Reeves, A., Taylor-Robinson, D., Barr, B., McKee, M. and Stuckler, D. (2015) 'Austerity, sanctions, and the rise of food banks in the UK', *The Bmj*, vol 350, p.h1775 (www.bmj.com/content/350/bmj.h1775).

Lynd, R.S. and Lynd, H.M. (1929) *Middletown*, New York: Harcourt, Brace & Company.

Lynd, R.S. and Lynd, H.M. (1937) *Middletown in transition*, New York: Harcourt, Brace & Company.

Macklin. R (2003) 'Dignity is a useless concept: It means no more than respect for persons or their autonomy', *British Medical Journal*, vol 327, pp 1419-20 (http://pubmedcentralcanada.ca/pmcc/articles/PMC300789/pdf/32701419.pdf).

Mantle, G. and Backwith, D. (2010) 'Poverty and social work', *British Journal of Social Work*, vol 40, pp 2380-97.

Marable, M. (2011) *Malcolm X: A life of reinvention*, London: Allen Lane.

Marmot, M. (Chair) (2010) *Fair society, healthy lives*, The Marmot Review, London: Department of Health (www.parliament.uk/documents/fair-society-healthy-lives-full-report.pdf).

Martin, J.P. (1985) *Hospitals in trouble*, Oxford: Blackwell.

Martinson, R. (1974) 'What works? Questions and answers about prison reform', *The public interest*, vol 35, p 22.

Mauer, M. (2006) *The race to incarcerate*, New York: New Press.

McArthur, M. and Winkworth, G. (2016) 'What do we know about the social networks of single parents who do not use supportive services?', *Child & Family Social Work*, doi: 10.1111/cfs.12278.

McDonald, L., Miller, H. and Sandler, J. (2015) 'A social ecological, relationship-based strategy for parent involvement: Families And Schools Together (FAST)', *Journal of Children's Services*, vol 10, issue 3, pp 218-30.

Mckenzie, L. (2015) *Getting by: Estates, class and culture in austerity Britain*, Bristol: Policy Press.

McNeill, F., Batchelor, S., Burnett, R. and Knox, J. (2005) *21st century social work: reducing re-offending-key practice skills*, Edinburgh: Scottish Executive.

Mead, L. (1992) *The new politics of poverty: The nonworking poor in America*, New York: Basic Books.

Milanovic, B. (2016) *Global inequality: A new approach for the age of globalization*, Cambridge, MA: Harvard University Press.

Mirowski, P. and Piehwe, D. (2015) *The road from Mont Pelerin: The making of the neoliberal thought collective*, Cambridge, MA: Harvard University Press.

Misztal, B.A. (2013) 'The idea of dignity: its modern significance', *European Journal of Social Theory*, vol 16, no 1, pp 101-21.

Monnickendam, M., Katz, C. and Monnickendam, M.S. (2010) 'Social workers serving poor clients: Perceptions of poverty and service policy', *British Journal of Social Work*, vol 40, pp 911-27.

Moore, C. (2014) *Margaret Thatcher: The authorized biography, Volume One: Not for turning*, London: Penguin.

Munro, E. (2010) *The Munro review of child protection interim report: The child's journey*, tri.x, Policy briefing 11 (www.trixonline.co.uk/website/news/pdf/policy_briefing_No-11.pdf).

Munro, E. (2011) *The Munro review of child protection: Final report, a child-centred system*, vol 8062), London: The Stationery Office.

Murray, C.A. (1990) *The emerging British underclass* (Choice in Welfare), London: Institute of Economic Affairs.

Murray, C.A. (1994) *Losing ground: American social policy, 1950-1980*, New York: Basic Books.

Murray, C.A. (2012) *Coming apart: The state of White America, 1960-2010*, New York: Random House.

Murray, R. (2016) 'Mistakes I have made in my research career', *Schizophrenia Bulletin*, vol 43, no 2, pp 253-56.

Myrdal, G. (1963) *Challenge to affluence*, New York: Pantheon.

Nardelli, A. and Arnett, G. (2015) 'Why are anti-immigration parties so strong in the Nordic states?', *The Guardian*, 19 June (www.theguardian.com/news/datablog/2015/jun/19/rightwing-anti-immigration-parties-nordic-countries-denmark-sweden-finland-norway).

Narey, M. (2014) *Making the education of social workers consistently effective: Report of Sir Martin Narey's independent review of the education of children's social workers*, London: DfE (www.gov.uk/government/publications/making-the-education-of-social-workers-consistently-effective).

Nayak, A. (2003) '"Boyz to men": Masculinities, schooling and labour transitions in de-industrial times', *Educational Review*, vol 55, issue 2, pp 147-59.

Newlin, M., Morris, D., Howarth, S. and Webber, M. (2015) 'Social participation interventions for adults with mental health problems: a review and narrative synthesis', *Social Work Research*, vol 39, no 3, pp 167-80.

Nietzsche, F. (1996) *On the genealogy of morals: A polemic: By way of clarification and supplement to my last book, Beyond good and evil* (Translated with an introduction and notes by Douglas Smith), Oxford: Oxford University Press.

Nietzsche, F. (1998) On the genealogy of morality, (Translated by Maudemarie Clark and Alan J. Swensen), Indianapolis, IN: Hackett.

Nozick, R. (1974) *Anarchy, state and utopia*, Oxford: Blackwell.

Oakley, A. (2005) *The Ann Oakley reader: Gender, women and social science*, Bristol: Policy Press.

Oakley, M. (2014) *Independent review of the operation of Jobseeker's Allowance sanctions validated by the Jobseekers Act 2013*, London: The Stationery Office (www.gov.uk/government/uploads/system/uploads/attachment_data/file/335144/jsa-sanctions-independent-review.pdf).

ODPM (Office of the Deputy Prime Minister) (2004) *Mental health and social exclusion*, London (www.nfao.org/Useful_Websites/MH_Social_Exclusion_report_summary.pdf).

Ofsted (2014) *Manchester City Council: Inspection 2014* (https://reports.ofsted.gov.uk/sites/default/files/documents/local_authority_reports/manchester/051_Single%20inspection%20of%20LA%20children's%20services%20and%20review%20of%20the%20LSCB%20as%20pdf.pdf).

O'Hara, M. (2015) *Austerity bites: A journey to the sharp end of cuts in the UK*, Bristol: Policy Press.

Olk, T. (2006) 'Welfare states and generational order', in H. Wintersberger, L. Alanen, T. Olk and J. Qvortrup (eds) *Childhood, generational order and the welfare state. Exploring children's social and economic welfare*, Odense: University of Southern Denmark Press, pp 59-90.

Omonira-Oyekanmi, R. (2014a) 'Black and dangerous? Listening to patients' experiences of mental health services in London' (www.opendemocracy.net).

Omonira-Oyekanmi, R. (2014b) *Town of stories* (https://rebeccaomonira.com/2014/11/12/town-of-stories/).

Orthner, D.K., Jones-Saupei, H. and Williamson, S. (2004) 'The resilience and strengths of low-income families', *Family Relations*, vol 53, pp 159-67.

Oxfam (2013) *Truth and lies about poverty: Ending comfortable myths about poverty*, Cardiff: Oxfam Cymru (http://policy-practice.oxfam.org. uk/publications/truth-and-lies-about-poverty-ending-comfortable-myths-about-poverty-306526).

Parrott, L. (2014) *Social work and poverty*, Bristol: Policy Press.

Parton, N. (2012) 'The Munro Review of child protection: An appraisal', *Children and Society*, vol 26, issue 2, pp 150-62.

Parton, N. (2014) *The politics of child protection: Contemporary developments and future directions*, Basingstoke: Palgrave Macmillan.

Peck, J. and Theodore, N. (2010) 'Recombinant workfare, across the Americas: Transnationalizing "fast" social policy', *Geoforum*, vol 41, issue 2, March, pp 195-208.

Peck, J. and Tickell, A. (2002) 'Neoliberalizing space', *Antipode*, vol 34, no 3, pp 380-404.

Pelton, L.H. (2015) 'The continuing role of material factors in child maltreatment and placement', *Child Abuse and Neglect*, vol 41, pp 30-9.

Perkins, A. (2016) 'The welfare trait: Hans Eysenck, personality and social issues', *Personality and Individual Differences*, vol 1, pp 172-8.

Perpich, D. (2008) *The ethics of Emmanuel Levinas*, Stanford, CA: Stanford University Press.

Philp, M. (1979) 'Notes on the form of knowledge in social work', *Sociological Review*, vol 27, no 1, pp 83-111.

Pierce, C. (1970) 'Offensive mechanisms', in F. Barbour (ed) *The Black seventies*, Boston, MA: Porter Sargent, pp 265-82.

Pierson, J. (2008) *Going local: Working in communities and neighbourhoods*, London: Routledge.

Piketty, T. (2015) *Capital in the 21st century*, Cambridge, MA: Harvard University Press.

Pinker, S. (2008) 'The stupidity of dignity', *The New Republic*, vol 238, no 9, pp 28-31.

Piven, F.F. and Cloward, R. (2012) *Regulating the poor: The functions of public welfare*, New York, NY: Vintage.

Pollitt, C. and Bouckaert, G. (1999) *Public management reform: A comparative analysis*, Oxford: Oxford University Press.

Rancière, J. (2004) *The philosopher and his poor*, Durham, NC: Duke University Press.

Rawls, J. (1971) *A theory of justice*, Cambridge, MA: Harvard University Press.

RCN (Royal College of Nursing) (2004) *Health and nursing care in the criminal justice service*, London (www.rcn.org.uk).

Reay, D. (2005) 'Beyond consciousness? The psychic landscape of social class', *Sociology*, vol 39, no 5, pp 911-28.

RITB (Recovery in the Bin) (no date) 'RITB – 20 key principles' (https://recoveryinthebin.org/recovery-in-the-bin-19-principless/).

Ritter, J.A. (2006) 'An empirical study evaluating the political participation of licensed social workers in the United States: A multi-state study', PhD dissertation, Austin, TX: The University of Texas at Austin.

Roberts, D.E. (1999) *Killing the black body: Race, reproduction, and the meaning of liberty*, New York, NY: Vintage Books.

Robinson, V., Andersson, A. and Musterd, S. (2003) *Spreading the 'burden'? A review of policies to disperse asylum seekers and refugees*, Bristol: Policy Press.

Rodger, J. (2008) *Criminalising social policy: Anti-social behaviour and welfare in a de-civilized society*, Cullompton: Willan.

Rose, N. (2007) *The politics of life itself*, New Haven, CT: Yale University Press.

Rossiter, A. (2011) 'Unsettled social work: The challenge of Levinas's ethics', *British Journal of Social Work*, vol 41, no 5, pp 980-95.

Rowntree, B. (2014) *Poverty: A study of town life* (Primary Source edn), Charleston, SC: Nabu Press.

Saar-Heiman, Y., Lavie-Ajayi, M. and Krumer-Nevo, M. (2017) 'Poverty-aware social work practice: service users' perspectives', *Child & Family Social Work*, vol 22, no 2, pp 1054-63.

Said, E. (1978) *Orientalism*, London: Penguin.

Salford City Council (no date) *Early identification, assessment of needs and intervention: A guide for practitioners*, Leeds: Children's Workforce Development Council, http://greatermanchesterscb.proceduresonline.com/pdfs/caf_guidance_practitioners.pdf

Sanchez-Jankowski, M. (2008) *Cracks in the pavement: Social change and resilience in poor neighborhoods*, Berkeley, CA: University of California Press.

Sandbrook, D. (2013) *Seasons in the sun: The battle for Britain, 1974-1979*, London: Penguin.

Sandel, M. (2009) *Justice: What's the right thing to do?*, London: Penguin.

Sanders, B. and Albanese, F. (2016) *"It's no life at all": Rough sleepers' experiences of violence and abuse on the streets of England and Wales*, London: Crisis (www.crisis.org.uk/media/20502/crisis_its_no_life_at_all2016.pdf).

Savage, M. (2015) *Social class in the 21st century*, London: Random House.

Savage, M. (2016) 'End class wars', *Nature*, vol 537, pp 475-8.

Savage, M., Bagnall, G. and Longhurst, B. (2001) 'Ordinary, ambivalent and defensive: Class identities in the Northwest of England', *Sociology*, vol 35, no 4, pp 875-92.

Savage, M., Devine, F., Cunningham, N., Taylor, M., Li, Y., Hjellbrekke, J. et al (2013) 'A new model of social class? Findings from the BBC's Great British Class Survey experiment', *Sociology*, vol 47, no 2, pp 219-50.

Sayer, A. (2005a) *The moral significance of class*, Cambridge: Cambridge University Press.

Sayer, A. (2005b) 'Class, moral worth and recognition', *Sociology*, vol 39, no 5, pp 947-63.

Sayer, A. (2015) *Why we can't afford the rich*, Bristol: Policy Press.

Scheff, T. (2003) 'Shame in self and society', *Symbolic Interaction*, vol 26, no 2, pp 239-62.

Scull, A. (2015) *Madness in civilization: A cultural history of insanity from the Bible to Freud, from the madhouse to modern medicine*, London: Thames & Hudson.

Seebohm, F. (1968) *Report of the Committee on Local Authority and Allied Social Services* (Cm3703), Her Majesty's Stationery Office.

Shildrick, T. and MacDonald, R. (2013) 'Poverty talk: how people experiencing poverty deny their poverty and why they blame "the poor"', *The Sociological Review*, vol 61, no 2, pp 285-303.

Sillitoe, A. (1958) *Saturday night and Sunday morning*, London: Fourth Estate.

Simon, J. (2007) *Governing through crime: How the war on crime transformed American democracy and created a culture of fear*, Oxford: Oxford University Press.

Simon, J. (2014) *Mass incarceration on trial: A remarkable court decision and the future of prisons in America*, New York: New Press.

Singer, P. (2006) 'Morality, reason, and the rights of animals', in F. Wals, S. Macedo and J. Ober (eds), *Primates and philosophers: how morality evolved*, Princeton, NJ: Princeton University Press, pp 140-60.

Skeggs, B. (2005) *Class, self and culture*, London: Routledge.

Skelcher, C. (2000) 'Changing images of the state: Overloaded, hollowed-out, congested', *Public Policy and Administration*, vol 15, no 3, pp 3-19.

Slater, T. (2009) '"Ghettos" and "anti-urbanism" entries', in R. Kitchin and N. Thrift (eds) *The international encyclopaedia of human geography*, London: Elsevier.

Slater, T. (2012) 'The myth of "broken Britain": Welfare reform and the production of ignorance', *Antipode*, pp 1-22.

Social Care Institute for Excellence (SCIE) (2010) *At a glance 26: Good practice in social care for refugees and asylum seekers*, London: SCIE (www.scie.org.uk/publications/ataglance/ataglance26.asp).

Standing, G. (2011) *The precariat: The new dangerous class*, London: Bloomsbury.

Stedman-Jones, D. (2012) *Masters of the universe: Hayek, Friedman, and the birth of neoliberal politics*, Oxford: Princeton University Press.

Stedman-Jones, G. (2004) *An end to poverty?*, London: Profile Books.

Stedman-Jones, G. (2013) *Outcast London*, London: Verso.

Stedman-Jones, G. (2014) *Outcast London: a study in the relationship between classes in Victorian society*, New York, NY: Verso Books.

Strier, R. and Binyamin, S. (2013) 'Introducing anti-oppressive social work practices in public services: Rhetoric to practice', *British Journal of Social Work*, pp 1-18.

Stuckler, D. and Basu, S. (2013) 'How austerity kills', *The New York Times*, 12 May (www.nytimes.com/2013/05/13/opinion/how-austerity-kills.html).

Subramanian, R. and Shames, A. (2013) *Sentencing and prison practices in Germany and the Netherlands: Implications for the United States*, New York: Vera Institute of Justice.

Swinford, S. (2016) 'Theresa May pledges to fight injustice and make Britain "a country that works for everyone" in her first speech as Prime Minister', *The Telegraph* (www.telegraph.co.uk/news/2016/07/13/theresa-mays-pledges-to-fight-injustice-and-make-britain-a-count/).

Taylor, C. (2003) *Modern social imaginaries*, Durham, NC: Duke University Press.

Taylor, D. (2016) 'Asylum seekers made to wear coloured wristbands in Cardiff', *The Guardian*, 24 January (www.theguardian.com/uk-news/2016/jan/24/asylum-seekers-made-to-wear-coloured-wristbands-cardiff).

The Equality Trust (nd) *How is economic inequality defined?* (www.equalitytrust.org.uk/how-economic-inequality-defined).

Thorpe, D., Regan, S., Mason, C. and May-Chahal, C. (2012) 'Making a case for common assessment framework responses to concerns about children', *Social Work and Social Sciences Review*, vol 12, no 3, pp 40-56.

Timmins, N. (1995) *The five giants: A biography of the welfare state*, London: HarperCollins.

Tirado, L. (2014) *Hand to mouth: The truth about being poor in a wealthy world*, London: Hachette UK.

Tobis, D. (2013) *From pariahs to partners: How parents and their allies changed New York City's child welfare system*, Oxford: Oxford University Press.

Todd, S. (2010) *The people: The rise and fall of the working class, 1910-2010*, London: John Murray.

Tonry, M. (1999) 'Why are US incarceration rates so high?', *Crime and Delinquency*, vol 45, pp 419-37.

Toynbee, P. and Walker, D. (2011) *The verdict: Did Labour change Britain?*, London: Granta.

Tyler, I. (2008) 'Chav mum, chav scum: Class disgust in contemporary Britain', *Feminist Media Studies*, vol 8, no 1, pp 17-34.

Tyler, I. (2013) *Revolting subjects: Social abjection and resistance in neoliberal Britain*, London: Zed Books.

United Nations Economic and Social Council (2016) 'Committee on Economic, Social and Cultural Rights: Concluding observations on the sixth periodic report of the United Kingdom of Great Britain and Northern Ireland', (http://tbinternet.ohchr.org/_layouts/treatybodyexternal/Download.aspx?symbolno=E/C.12/GBR/CO/6&Lang=En).

United Nations General Assembly (1948) *Universal declaration of human rights*, UN General Assembly.

United Nations General Assembly (2012) 'Final Draft of the Guiding Principles on Extreme Poverty and Human Rights', Submitted by the Special Rapporteur on extreme poverty and human rights, Magdalena Sepúlveda Carmona (http://daccess-dds-ny.un.org/doc/UNDOC/GEN/G12/154/60/PDF/G1215460.pdf?OpenElement).

Wacquant, L. (2004) *Body and soul: Ethnographic notebooks of an apprentice boxer*, Oxford: Oxford University Press.

Wacquant, L. (2007) 'Territorial stigmatization in the age of advanced marginality', *Thesis Eleven*, vol 91, no 1, pp 66-77.

Wacquant, L. (2008a) 'Ghettos and anti-ghettos: An anatomy of the new urban poverty', *Thesis Eleven*, vol 94, pp 113-18.

Wacquant, L. (2008b) *Urban outcasts: A comparative sociology of advanced marginality*, Cambridge: Polity Press.

Wacquant, L. (2009a) *Prisons of poverty*, Minneapolis, MS: University of Minnesota Press.

Wacquant, L. (2009b) *Punishing the poor: The neoliberal government of social insecurity*, Durham, NC: Duke University Press.

Wacquant, L. (2010) 'Class, race and hyperincarceration in revanchist America', *Daedalus*, vol 139, no 3, pp 74-90.

Wacquant, L. (2012) 'Three steps to a historical anthropology of actually existing neoliberalism', *Social Anthropology*, vol 20, no 1, pp 66-79.

Waldron, J. (2007) 'Dignity and rank', *Archive Européenne de Sociologie*, vol XLVIII, pp 201-37.

Walmsley, R. (2015) *World female imprisonment list* (3rd edn), International Centre for Prison Studies (www.prisonstudies.org/sites/default/files/resources/downloads/world_female_imprisonment_list_third_edition_0.pdf).

Warner, J. (2013) 'Social work, class politics and risk in the moral panic over Baby P', *Health, Risk & Society*, vol 15, issue 3.

Warner, J. (2015) *The emotional politics of social work and child protection*, Bristol: Policy Press.

Webb, S. (2009) 'Against difference and diversity in social work: The case of human rights', *International Journal of Social Welfare*, vol 18, issue 3, pp 307-16.

Webb, S. (2010) '(Re)Assembling the Left: The politics of redistribution and recognition in social work', *British Journal of Social Work*, vol 40, pp 2364-79.

Webb, S.A. and Gray, M. (eds) (2013) *The new politics of social work*, Basingstoke: Palgrave Macmillan.

Webber, M., Corker, E., Hamilton, S., Weeks, C., Pinfold, V., Rose, D. et al (2014) 'Discrimination against people with severe mental health illness and their access to social capital: Findings from the Viewpoint Survey', *Epidemiology and Psychiatric Sciences*, vol 23, no 2, pp 155-65.

Welshman, J. (2013) *Underclass: A history of the excluded since 1880*, London: Bloomsbury.

White, V. (2009) 'Quiet challenges? Professional practice in modernised social work', in J. Harris and V. White (eds) *Modernising social work: Critical considerations*, Bristol: Policy Press, Chapter 7.

WHO (World Health Organization) (2007) *Trenčín statement* (www.euro.who.int/__data/assets/pdf_file/0006/99006/E91402.pdf).

WHO (2012) 'Social determinants of health' (www.who.int/social_determinants/sdh_definition/en/).

WHO (2013) *TB and prisons: WHO global report 2013* (www.who.int/tb/areas-of-work/population-groups/global_report_prisons_2013.pdf?).

WHO (2014) 'Mental health: a state of well-being', WHO (www.who.int/features/factfiles/mental_health/en/).

Wiesel, E. (1992) 'Foreword', in G.J. Annas and M.A. Grodin, *The Nazi doctors and the Nuremberg Code Human rights in human experimentation*, Oxford: Oxford University Press, pp i-ix.

Wilkinson, R. (2000) *Mind the gap: Hierarchies, health and human evolution*, London: Weidenfeld & Nicolson.

Wilkinson, R. and Pickett, K. (2009) *The spirit level: Why equality is better for everyone*, London: Penguin.

Williams, R. (2014) *Keywords: A vocabulary of culture and society*, London: Fourth Estate.

Willis, P. (2000) *Learning to labour: How working class kids get working class jobs*, Farnham: Ashgate.

Wilson, W.J. (1996) *When work disappears: The world of the new urban poor*, New York, NY: Alfred A Knopf.

Wilson, W.J. (2012) *The truly disadvantaged: The inner city, the underclass, and public policy*, Chicago, IL: University of Chicago Press.

Woolf, Lord Justice (1991) *Prison disturbances April 1990: Report of an inquiry*, London: HMSO.

Yeates, N. (2002) 'Globalization and social policy: from global neoliberal hegemony to global political pluralism', *Global Social Policy*, vol 2, no 1, pp 69-91.

Young, H. (2013) *One of us* (final edn), London: Pan Books.

Young, M. (1958) *The Rise of the meritocracy*, Harmondsworth: Penguin.

Young, M. (2001) 'Down with meritocracy', *The Guardian*, 29 June (www.theguardian.com/politics/2001/jun/29/comment).

Young, M. (2004) *The rise of the meritocracy* (2nd revised edn), London: Transaction Books.

Younge, G. (2017) 'The cause of death that dare not speak its name: austerity', *The Guardian*, 15 April (www.theguardian.com/membership/commentisfree/2017/apr/15/knife-crime-cause-death-dare-not-speak-name-austerity-cuts-youth-funding).

Index